D1100616

OLIVER REED:
TEN TOP MOVIES
By Andy Black
ISBN 1 902588 06 1
Published by
THE GLITTERBOOKS OF LONDON
Copyright © Andy Black 1999
All world rights reserved

CONTENTS

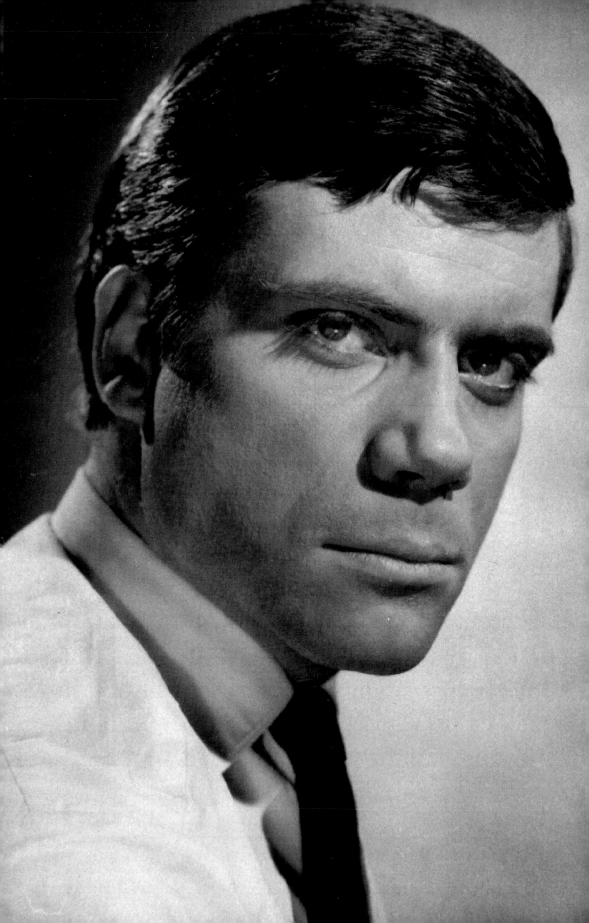

INTRODUCTION

"Michael [Winner] gave me my money, and [Ken] Russell gave me my art. But Hammer gave me my technique."

From his formative years spent pulling down his cousin Vicky's knickers while playing doctors and nurses, as her mother entered the room when he was only 5 (Vicky growing up to become Samantha Eggar, his eventual co-star in **The Brood**), to his first film role opposite Sonja Henie in **Hello London** (1958) – "I was disappointed in Sonja Henie. Her legs were muscle-bound and unattractive and didn't give me the urge to give her one" – to his final moments on 2 May 1999 in Valletta, Malta when he lay stretched out on a bar room floor giggling with chest pains, whilst filming what was to be his last role as Proximo in Ridley Scott's **Gladiator** (1999), Oliver Reed lapped up the life and lived the dream as prolific drinker, serial seducer of women and hellraiser *par excellence*.

That his later years were increasingly dominated not by his work but by his stumbling, drunken appearances on numerous TV chat shows, is something which yes, to a degree, he actively cultivated and which the mischievous rogue in him would no doubt have appreciated. But to let such sordid forays and intoxicated antics obscure his memorable film career? No, not even the compulsive partygoer and hedonistic Olly would welcome that, not after such a rich and varied career which encompassed nearly 100 films and spanned some 40 years in total.

Although Reed initially began to make a name in Hammer horror movies, the vast majority of his work came after his now trademark facial scars appeared – the result of being attacked

The System

with a broken glass in The Crazy Elephant nightclub in London shortly after filming Michael Winner's **The System** in 1966. Ironically, his horror roles actually *decreased* afterwards, despite the added physical piquancy he now naturally had for such roles.

In the early 1960s Reed struggled with the vagaries of the acting profession, especially the sporadic nature of the work. Due to his looks, his appearances were generally limited to background roles as Teddy Boys, nightclub bouncers, or other moody young men in the likes of **Beat Girl** or Tony Hancock's **The Rebel**. Then, after bit parts in the 1960 Hammer productions **The Two Faces Of Dr Jekyll** and **Sword Of**

The Shuttered Room

Sherwood Forest, he was given his first stab at a starring role by the company, being cast as Leon in **Curse Of The Werewolf** (1961). His other Hammer roles would include the smuggler Harry in **Captain Clegg** (1962), pirate Brocaire in **Pirates Of Blood River** (1962), biker King in **The Damned** (1963), soldier Sylvester in **The Scarlet Blade** (1963), psychopath Simon Ashby in **Paranoiac** (1963), and rebel leader Eli Khan in **The Brigand Of Kandahar** (1965) – the latter regarded by the actor as his worst film for Hammer. This trait for playing rogues and psychopaths extended to his roles as the brutish fur-trapper La Bete in

Sidney Hayers' **The Trap**, shot in the wilds of Canada and co-starring Rita Tushingham, and as the New England bully terrorising Flora Robson in David Greene's adaptation of H P Lovecraft's **The Shuttered Room**.

After the aforementioned glassing incident, Reed now had the added obstacle of his scarred features. It was extrovert director Ken Russell who was ultimately to pluck Reed from the obscurity of the assorted jobs he undertook in order to eke out an existence; mini-cab driver, strip-club bouncer and hospital porter being among the diverse collection he tried his hand at, with only a phone call from Hammer saving him from the ignominy of becoming a vacuum cleaner salesman on another occasion. Russell's TV project *The Debussy Film* gave Reed the chance to display sensitivity as an actor, something his previous roles had denied him.

"I regard *Debussy* as the turning point in my career. It was the point at which I began to shoot upwards, sometimes, though not always, away from the cast of villains that I was poured into for my earlier roles," Reed explained when considering the importance of Russell's influence upon his career.

Given Reed's apparently continual collision course with life, with the many fights and scrapes he survived, it's perhaps appropriate that his introduction into the world – he was born in Wimbledon, South London on February 13 1938 – was courtesy of his father Peter – a Civil Defence ambulance driver and also ambulance driver during the Second World War – and his mother Marcia.

Growing up as he did, in the shadow of the war, much of Reed's early years were spent in a Morrison shelter, dodging the

German air raids with his cushions and pillows for company and reading A A Milne's *Winnie The Pooh* under the light of a bicycle lamp.

With a natural reticence towards blood, the young Reed was classed as a veggie, humorously, when considering his later bar room exploits and given that he was also a bastard descendant of the notorious Russian monarch Peter Romanoff – Peter the Great, who shed more blood than virtually any other monarch in history, including personally beheading 200 mutineers during the rebel march on Moscow. (It is also interesting to note the physical similarities between the monarch's own death's head mask and Reed's own features when portraying the role of the shaven-headed priest Grandier in **The Devils**).

Having negotiated his 2 years' National Service in the Army based in Aldershot, Reed's acting talents began seeking an outlet – not for him the pretence of drama school or the artifice of acting class, rather that: "My acting school was and still is, life in the raw, the whole wide world as a stage." He continues: "I didn't go into a shop full of mirrors, I stayed outside and gazed at the reflections of life," finally concluding that: "I've got a lot of performances stored away at the back of my mind, ready to come out in front of the cameras when they are needed."

Reed's one very tangible link however with the world of film came from within his own family, via his Granny May giving Grandfather Sir Herbert Beerbohm Tree no less than six "love" children, including the famous film director Sir Carol Reed.

Oliver was to seek advice and encouragement from his illustrious relative throughout his career, most notably reflected

when John Woolf and his Uncle asked him to play the part of Bill Sykes in Lionel Bart's musical version of **Oliver!** (1968). It was during this time, also notable for Reed's role opposite Diana Rigg in **The Assassination Bureau**, that he met and fell in love with his eventual second wife, dancer Jacquie Daryl.

Having kick-started his career with the aforementioned **Hello London**, Reed followed this up with a role as an extra in the Norman Wisdom vehicle **The Square Peg** (1958), before later delivering his first speech lines in TV series *The Four Just Men* (1959) when filling in for another actor who went absent. He was rewarded with the princely sum of £12 for his efforts, which enabled Reed to pay off two weeks of rent arrears!

Then followed Reed's Hammer period. It was a bout of meningitis hospitalising him during this time which was to force Reed's hand in choosing his first wife, Kate, when his two girlfriends ended up visiting him at the same time – make your mind up time indeed was the ultimatum he was given.

Having duly married Kate on New Year's Day, 1960 at Kensington Registry Office, their union was to produce the birth of Reed's son, Mark.

Just before Reed was to embark on his pivotal film partnership with Michael Winner, he had an impromptu audition for a film by director Elia Kazan, who had previously made some of the James Dean films that Reed so admired and whose anecdotes struck a chord with him instantly. Kazan told him that, frustrated at the virgin drinker Dean's inability to play a drunk on a rooftop required for one scene, he bought him two bottles of bourbon and told him to go away and keep drinking for two days, whereupon Dean duly returned only to play the scene perfectly. Kazan eventually passed over Reed for the part – but he sounded like a dream director for Olly!

His eventual work with Winner, which was to ultimately prove so important, got off to a similarly faltering start. Whilst Winner proposed Reed for the lead role in his latest film **West 11** (1963) opposite Julie Christie, the film's producer had other plans. As Reed himself revealed: "Danny Angel said Christie was a B-picture artist and I was a *nothing* – but Danny Angel couldn't walk so I couldn't knock him over." The roles subsequently went to Alfred Lynch and Kathleen Breck.

But, thankfully, Winner persisted and Reed did get to star in his next film **The System**, being the first of several collaborations between the two. Although confessing how Winner's arrogance and love of the megaphone while directing can present a boorish face to many, Alfred Hitchcock's assertion that "actors are cattle" was countered by Winner thus: "Show me a cow who can earn a million dollars a film..." Reed later confided: "I like Winner because he loves actors."

Of Reed's other seminal influence, Ken Russell, he explained their meeting regarding *The Debussy Film* for the BBC *Omnibus* series, Reed now brandishing his distinctive scars. "What about the scars?" Reed asked. "What scars?" being Russell's reply, the director continuing: "Anyway, you'll be wearing a beard."

It was while filming *Debussy* in France that these two reprobates indulged in some mutual fun and games. On one occasion, having chosen to eat at an expensive restaurant, Russell, Reed and most of the cast and crew members bought only one bottle of wine from the extortionate wine list, proceeding to smuggle in under their table, cheaper bottles which Reed and Russell had bought from a wine shop earlier. As the group begun to get progressively drunk, the female members carried away the empties in their handbags in trips to the toilet whilst the proprietor puzzled over how so many people could be drunk on such a small quantity of wine!

In a later visit to another restaurant, Reed and Russell, taking pity on the live fish swimming around in the restaurant's own fish/menu tank, proceeded to emancipate the fish by picking them out of the tank and then releasing them into a nearby stream – an act they later had to pay for!

This altruistic side of Russell wasn't always so apparent however, as Reed recalled being left battered and bruised (and cold) from the infamous nude wrestling scene in **Women In Love**, as for take after take, he and co-star Alan Bates kept hitting the hard stone floor (Russell found the foam-backed section they were supposed to be using just too unrealistic). "Russell is a Jekyll and Hyde. As a man, I adore him, but he can become a monster on set", Reed's view being reinforced during the filming of **The Devils** where Russell insisted upon Reed having to have his eyebrows shaved off. Reed capitulated, but only after heavily insuring himself against possible non-regrowth.

After **Women In Love**, Reed was to star with Glenda Jackson once more in Michael Apted's **The Triple Echo** (1971). Reed would later comment: "Glenda is a fantastic actress. Put her in gear on screen and she's like a Bedford truck. She will run all over you." He starred with another great actress, the legendary Bette Davis, in the ghost story **Burnt Offering** (1976). Other notable films of this period included the brutal British crime thriller **Sitting Target, The Hunting Party** with Gene Hackman, Andrew Sinclair's bizarre black magic arthouse entry **Blue Blood**,

Burnt Offering

the totalitarian sci-fi tale **Z.P.G. (Zero Population Growth)**, and Richard Lester's **The Three Musketeers** – which latter led to Reed's continued typecasting in such period dramas as **Royal Flash** and **The Prince And The Pauper**.

Reed's last film for Ken Russell – Russell's monstrous adaptation of The Who's rock opera **Tommy** – led to his infamous friendship with drummer and fellow hellraiser Keith Moon. Moon landed, uninvited, by helicopter in the grounds of Broome Hall – the sixty-three bedroom Victorian mansion in Surrey which Olly had bought in 1970, ostensibly to stable his horse, Dougal. Thus commenced a friendship marked by alcoholic excess and hotel-wrecking exploits involving Moon's usual retinue of groupies and Swedish models, which continued

Tommy

until the drummer's untimely death.

One of Reed's favourite challenges was his "unofficial" drinking contest with his US counterpart Lee Marvin before they began shooting **The Great Scout And Cathouse Thursday** (1976) in Mexico. Refereed by noted US character actor Strother Martin, they began downing vodkas – their chosen "weapon" – before Reed eventually triumphed after many hours to take the trophy – or Marvin's "drinking cloak" at any rate – with cloak nearly being followed by dagger from the irate Mexican locals they succeeded in offending! Marvin's impression upon first seeing Reed at their hotel: "I was expecting to meet up with this actor who was supposed to be Britain's hellraiser and what do I see but this tailor's dummy in a pinstripe suit looking more like a fucking banker." But he soon knew the truth.

At least here the liquor went down Reed's throat, whereas his appearance on the Johnny Carson TV show in America with Shelley Winters led to whisky being poured over Reed – retaliation for his remarks about his co-guest's "Hitler moustache" in an intimate place!

Reed met another Hollywood drinking legend, Robert Mitchum, on the set of Michael Winner's **The Big Sleep**. There is no report of another contest, but Olly later recalled Mitchum downing a whole bottle of gin in fifty-five minutes.

Many of Reed's appearances (not always public) have been equally dramatic; including removing his trousers live on the *Saturday Night At The Mill* TV show, punching the best man at his brother David's wedding and simultaneously also removing the unfortunate victim's wig, to celebrating David's (again) birthday and landing up with an £8,000 bill for hotel damage, a naked girl jumping out of the giant birthday cake and Reed wrestling with Ringo Starr just some of the other incidental highlights.

Reed also made some kind of history by appearing on the popular Radio 4 show, *Desert Island Discs* with host Roy Plomley and selecting, not say Brahms and Liszt as his musical choices but the likes of Pooh Bear's "Honey Song" and "Did You Ever See An Elephant Fly" by Louis Armstrong.

All very much child's play when compared to one of Olly's infamous stag nights, which began by climbing up the chimney of The Cricketers Arms in Ockley and then dancing naked inside with his 45 invited guests from Rosslyn Park Rugby club, singing

Olly at Broome Hall

"Get 'em down, you Zulu Warriors" and eating fairy cakes iced in the club's colours, cramming 15 men into one ladies toilet cubicle, before embarking on a near-naked cross country run to Olly's beloved estate Broome Hall, via the lake!

With his then second wife Jacquie and her friends safely locked away upstairs for the Saturday evening and Sunday morning, Olly and his pals then proceeded to demolish a 50 gallon beer keg between them, plus 32 bottles of scotch, 17 bottles of gin, 4 crates of wine and 15 dozen bottles of Newcastle Brown Ale!

Whether this quantity beats Olly's alleged personal record of 104 pints in one extended session is unclear!

As wife (and mother of their daughter Sarah) Jacquie calmly recalled: "It could've been worse. I suppose a lot of them were in training and off the drink." She further commented of her husband: "If I heard he'd run off to Siberia with Brigitte Bardot, I wouldn't bat an eyelid. What's the point? If he wants to do that, there seems no point in trying to stop him. I realise I don't think in conventional terms about marriage, but then I suppose I'm not normal in so far as no normal female would ever get involved with Oliver."

When Oliver Reed married for a third time, it was to a girl some twenty years his junior. Josephine Burge was just 17 when their relationship started. This was at the turn of the 1980s, a point when Reed had snubbed the chance of Hollywood stardom, and the subsequent decline of the British film industry gradually saw him relegated to character roles in lower budget features and TV movies, only enlivened by the occasional gem such as Nic Roeg's **Castaway** or Terry Gilliam's **Baron Munchausen** (in which Reed played Vulcan, the god of fire). Olly became known less for his screen roles than for his inebriated TV appearances (for example his legendary stint on cult youth program *The Word*, performing a bizarre rendition of The Troggs' "Wild Thing") and drunken brawling. Finally, his downturn in fortune led to the inevitable sale of Broome Hall, and he relocated to a farmstead in Ireland.

It was here that Oliver Reed was finally laid to rest – a stone's throw from his favourite pub – in May 1999. As his brother succinctly put it: "He could have been a star, but he chose life instead".

CURSE OF THE WEREWOLF

"The blood. There was blood on my hands.
Where did I get the blood?"
—Leon (Oliver Reed)

Being a mere 22 years old at the time, and chosen from 17 other hopefuls, Terence Fisher's **Curse Of The Werewolf** (1961) was to be *the* film that launched Oliver Reed's hitherto fledgling acting career and so catapulted him on the road to celluloid stardom.

The film, one of Hammer's most controversial, was to be Reed's first of several collaborations with the company, which also stretched further to include **The Pirates Of Blood River** (1962), **The Damned** (1963), and **Paranoiac** (1964), amongst others.

Reed's opinion of **Curse** was considerably more favourable however, as the reported £90 a week wages represented a "fortune" for the time, enabling the then struggling actor to both "pay the rent *and* have a beer".

Such was the impact of Reed's dual, tortured role as the youthful Leon, continually battling to suppress the "beast inside" – the werewolf of the title – that following the film's release Reed fan clubs sprang up all over the world, including America, Italy and France, with over 50 marriage proposals being mailed to the emerging actor!

The evolution of **Curse** from script to screen was to be far removed however, from any such marital bliss, instead falling foul of the social and political constraints of the time – more so than any other entry in Hammer's blood-drenched history.

With Hammer originally due to begin shooting an ambitious period study in terror, "The Inquisitor" (aka "The Rape Of Sabena") – set in a small Spanish town gripped by the Inquisition and starring Philip Latham and Kieron Moore – co-producers Columbia were to strangle the film, abruptly, in its infancy.

Fearing public condemnation over the religious polemics within the story from the (then) persuasive Catholic church body, the Legion of Decency – and not least the tangible threat of the film being banned – not for the first time did set designer Bernard Robinson have to utilise his reserves of ingenuity by cannibalising the "Inquisitor" sets for use in the (marginally) less controversial **Curse**.

Using Anthony Hind's (writing under his Hammer pseudonym John Elder) script based upon Guy Endore's renowned novel, *The Werewolf Of Paris*, so was **Curse** born, only now set in the Spanish town of Santa Vera in 1560 and centring around Leon's doomed love for Christina (Catherine Feller), whose continual love he requires in order to conquer the lycanthropic urges which rear up inside him.

Director Fisher's assertion that "I consider it to be a tragic love story and not fundamentally a 'horror story'", unfortunately wasn't shared by the censor of the period, John Trevelyan.

Although Hammer considered themselves to have had a good rapport hitherto with the BBFC, **Curse** was to prove a glaring exception with over 14 cuts in total, including 2 entire sequences being removed due to **Curse** being the first "sexy" werewolf picture – blatantly linking wolfdom with wanton sexuality with Leon's ensuing savagery being symbolically awakened during his visit to a brothel.

As Trevelyan explained at the time, **Curse** was the first of Hammer's gothic entries to mix the dual taboos – the "dangerous cocktail" of horror and sex. Most problematic of all the scenes proved to be the rape of a servant girl (Yvonne Romain) by a beggar (Richard Wordsworth), leaving the girl pregnant with Leon (the baby being born on Christmas day) – its first action being to bite its mother's finger, signalling its demonic personality.

Censorial propriety allowing for horror or sex, but not both in the same scene, we see the beggar's profuse body hair betraying signs of his lycanthropy as he attacks and rapes the girl (off screen).

Fisher may have asserted the "romantic" overtones he sought to imbue the film with, but in this pivotal scene he leaves little to the imagination by way of Romain's low-cut dress and ample cleavage, continuing the "gratuity" in her subsequent frenzied stabbing of a lecherous assailant in the chest (one of the scenes severely cut).

As time moves on following baby Leon's birth, we see the ominous portents provided by his baptism as the sun begins to fade through the stained glass windows of the church and the water in the font begins to foam and bubble, thunder simultaneously rumbling outside.

With lambs and chickens being mysteriously slaughtered by a wolf-like creature, the local nightwatchman Pepe (Warren Mitchell) says ironically of the young Leon (played by Justin Walters): "He can't stand the sight of blood", little realising that

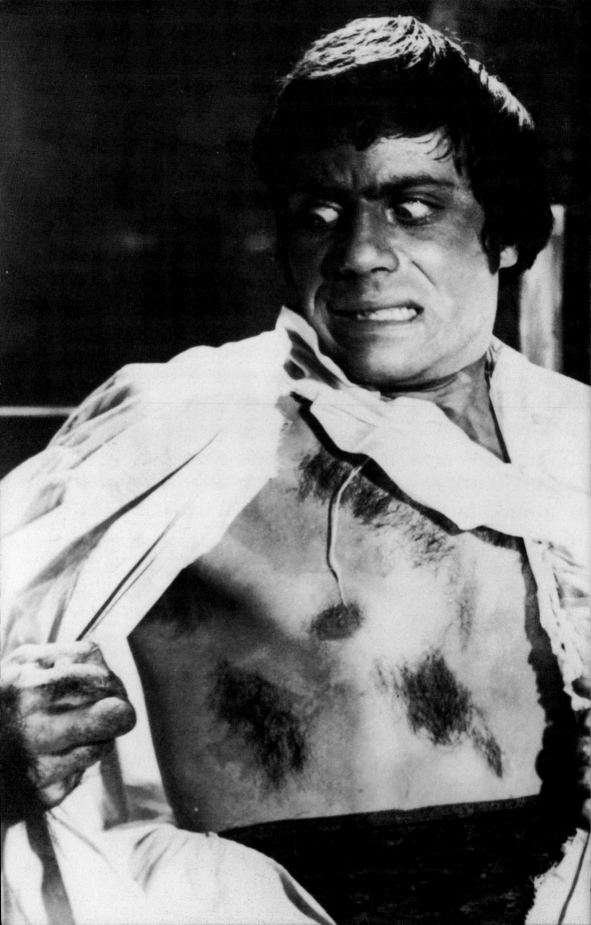

the boy's timid nature is only external, concealing a raging beast inside.

As the true horrifying nature of Leon's condition gradually begins to dawn on his surrogate parents, led by the kindly Alfredo (Clifford Evans), the sight of the young boy clutching at the bars on his bedroom window, staring intently at the full moon outside, his teeth now fanged, creates a chilling tableaux.

As the local priest surmises: "A werewolf is a body where the soul and spirit are constantly at war. The spirit is that of a wolf. And whatever weakens the human soul – vice, greed, hatred, solitude, especially during the cycle of the full moon when the forces of evil are at their strongest – these bring the spirit of the wolf to the fore. And in turn, whatever weakens the spirit of the beast – warmth, fellowship, love – raise the human soul".

With the passage of time now delineating the progress of Leon from young boy to young man (now played by Reed), the innermost angst and turmoil of the lycanthropic condition is now evident for all to see. Having begun to work for Christina's father in his wine company, Leon's blossoming relationship with her severely irks Christina's father. The two lovers are drawn closer together – "It's just a dream," Christina opines in response to Leon's marriage proposal; "No, this is real Christina," being Leon's firm, heart-felt reply.

With only Christina's love standing between him and the oblivion which self-destruction will bring, Leon is persuaded to visit the local brothel one night and it is here that his lupine nature surfaces with a vengeance – having been taken upstairs by a prostitute only for him to bite her shoulder – and the action then rapidly cuts to his now profusely-haired arm

grabbing her by the neck, only for the severely truncated scene to end – Leon's savage brutality consigned to the cutting room floor.

The following morning Leon awakes at home, unsure of his murderous actions the night before but with his hands covered in blood. "I can't remember anything," he laments, begging the priest for guidance. "What am I going to do father?".

The priest's response that he must chain himself up in his room securely for his own safety and that of others, meets with an emotional response: "Oh yes, that's right. You chain up wild animals, and that's all I am. A wild animal". Only Christina's love and affection in caring for him and staying with Leon through the troublesome night avert his beastly transformation.

Sensing how he is tearing Christina apart emotionally – and perhaps even endangering her – Leon then reverts to the notion of being imprisoned, or worse; "Tell him I confess. Tell him I must be executed now, before sunset!" he shouts from his prison cell as the approaching mayor arrives to sentence him.

In a state of absolute turmoil, Leon turns to his father and begs him: "Father, Pepe the nightwatchman has a silver bullet. Get it and use it. Use it on me father. You must use it on me".

These prophetic words prove to be Leon's epitaph as the moon emerges outside to provide the catalyst for his transformation into his werewolf self – his hands rapidly growing hair, shirt ripping and face contorting into a snarling, bloodshot-eyed animal. His ensuing escape from his cell leads to the final confrontation with the locals, as Leon leaps across the rooftops, chased by the torch-wielding mob below baying for his blood. Ultimately, it is left to his guardian to corner him at the top of the bell tower and dispatch the fatal bullet, to end Leon's life but also his external misery – a mercy killing in every sense of the word.

Whilst Reed's dual performance of a tortured human soul, whose pursuit of true love is forever doomed by his animalistic "other" is central to the film's success and our enjoyment of it, **Curse** also benefits from Hind's script which shifts the action from the source novel's France to rural Spain, so gaining from the pervading religious dynamics of the region, which underpins the emotional core and horror trappings of the film.

Though the film's troubled history and near legendary cuts (the US release being 3 minutes longer than the UK version and even coinciding with the school holiday period in the States!), render **Curse** the nearest Hammer ever came to having a bona fide "cult" film, the rather simplistic "love" element detracts somewhat from the potentially more interesting social evils that are perpetrated as opposed to the metaphysical ones.

The *true* evil here is not Reed's transmogrified Leon as much as the arrogant aristocrats who control the social order with no room for compassion or love. As the locals debate the Marque's impending marriage at the beginning of the film, the truth is revealed: "Who'll have to pay for this wedding? We shall. Who's paid for the bride? We have. And who's paying for the feast that's going on at this very moment up at the castle? We are".

The beggar's own subsequent journey to the castle in search of mercy proves to be ultimately fruitless as the mocking aristocrats humiliate their servants before then "buying" Wordsworth's blind beggar as if a pet animal and then encouraging him to get drunk in order to provide amusement for the party.

With compassion defunct and love redundant – a notion confirmed in the caricature of "love" offered up by the prostitute who provokes Leon's animalistic response – we see **Curse** delineating the patriarchal evil which Fisher portrays as the sins of the fathers are visited upon their sons (as opposed

to, say, the matriarchal evil Fisher shows in **The Gorgon** [1964], where the titular female adversary represents the dominant evil).

In the final analysis, the rather one-dimensional supporting characters lack the necessary substance to reinforce some of the film's more subtle but vital nuances, and as such **Curse** probably falls just short of being the classic it is often vaunted to be. It nonetheless remains probably the best werewolf movie to date (comparisons with its nearest rival, Joe Dante's **The Howling**, being virtually impossible due to the stylistic differences).

As for Reed, given that he only occupies barely half the film in terms of screen-time (and half of that buried under fur), his emotive performance remains memorable. As he himself fondly recalls: "To think of the **Werewolf** – I was 22. And to *see* this young fellow striding down the road, whistling... and throwing stones. Black hair, lean body. You never grow old when you've got that".

And to reaffirm his startling entrance into the cinema and his subsequent elevation in status, Reed confided that "After **Werewolf** I was asked to dine with the directors. Then you *knew* you'd made it, because that's where Christopher (Lee) and Peter (Cushing) were".

THE DAMNED

"Look Joanie. It's you and me against the world,
just like it's always been"
—King (Oliver Reed) to his sister Joan (Shirley Anne Field)

Along with Hammer's own **Quatermass** series of sci-fi films, **The Damned** (US title: **These Are The Damned**) has been dubbed as one of the highlights of the early British post-war sci-fi films period, under the capable guiding hand of celebrated American director Joseph Losey, whose previous films had included **The Boy With Green Hair** (1948) and **M** (1951).

Given the cerebral quality which Losey could bring to this politically controversial project, and the fact that Losey was virtually ostracised from the Hollywood system at the time, being "tarnished" as a Communist sympathiser during the McCarthy witch hunt era, Hammer's offer to direct the film in the UK was well timed.

Adapted from H L Lawrence's source novel *The Children Of The Light*, the central premise for **The Damned** revolves around the misguided attempts of a scientist Bernard (Alexander Knox), to raise his own coterie of surrogate children in a subterranean hideaway in order that they be able to survive the nuclear war he fears is inevitable.

The fact that in the process, he has isolated the children from their natural parents in pursuit of his own personal post-nuclear ideology/utopia, fails to trigger any feelings of remorse or guilt in Bernard. His "children" are taught remotely via close circuit TV screens which link to their underground classroom, which in reality becomes their prison.

This chilling, wholly impersonal approach provides the boundaries of demarcation whereby success is not a visionary, celebratory pursuit but merely the selfish conceit of an uncaring idealist. Ironically, for a film of this sci-fi-aligned persuasion, the typical roles are reversed as it is the artist, represented here by Freya (Viveca Lindfors), who is transmuted as the visionary – her abstract, bird-like sculptures chillingly representing the charred bodies which a nuclear war would inevitably bring.

Despite this engaging premise and compelling nuances, the film does rather stumble in its attempts to merge too many genres within its pot-pourri structure – as elements of romance, teen-gang and sci-fi uneasily combine.

Oliver Reed's motorcycle-gang leader King, is introduced as a hard-nosed rogue, his rather dapper appearance – clean shaven with checked jacket, white shirt and black tie – at times appearing aloof from the thuggery his gang initiates. "Forward into battle dear chaps" is King's "war cry" to his leather-clad troops, who utilise King's sister Joan (Shirley Anne Field) and her feminine wiles – clad provocatively in a clingy sweater top – in order to entice unsuspecting victims who are then summarily mugged.

When a wealthy American tourist Simon Wells (Macdonald Carey) is attacked by the gang in the coastal town of Weymouth, King has a "watching" brief – casually whistling as the beating is perpetrated, a contrasting image used to great effect later in Stanley Kubrick's **A Clockwork Orange** (1971).

"The age of senseless violence has caught up with us too," is Bernard's response to the crime whilst also perhaps signalling the erosion of the social fabric of society from the outset – as dysfunctional, disaffected characters, we see King and his gang aimlessly killing time in the local amusements arcades. In view of this, the advent of Bernard's anticipated global war and the resultant devastation may not be that far in the future after all.

King's aggressive streak later manifests itself when Wells happens to meet up with Joan again aboard his boat moored in the quay – King admonishing his sister thus: "Don't ever do that again. Do you think I'm going to let a man put his dirty hands on you?". King's obsessive "protection" of his sister, betraying a latent trace of incestuous feelings, possibly resulted we learn, from him locking his sister up in a cupboard on one occasion when she was twenty years old, after she had tried to go out with a prospective boyfriend.

When Wells and Joan escape on his boat, heading for the same remote coastal locale which, it later transpires, houses the children, King follows and searches for them having tracked them to Freya's cliff-top cottage – densely populated by the macabre sculptures she creates.

As Freya returns home to discover her intruder, King berates her: "I know your kind. Smart talking, bad living. People with no morals." He continues his diatribe against her by pointing accusingly at her sculptures – "You think this junk's all that matters," before summarily taking an axe to the objects d'art and routinely smashing them (foreshadowing the opening scenes of **I'll Never Forget Whatsisname** a few years later).

It is here that King's complex character and hidden motives begin to emerge in self-revelatory style before our eyes. He changes before us from loutish outcast to an idealistic, almost moralistic crusader, subverting his various character foibles in a display of manic rage and frustration.

"How could you be so cruel to me," the now distraught Freya pleads, with "I enjoyed it my lady," being King's cold, ambiguous reply as he moves from an anti-materialistic, social thinker on the one hand, to impetuous luddite on the other.

His transition into a well-rounded "good-guy" appears complete as he reluctantly (at first) buries the hatchet with Wells, when he encounters him and Joan in the coastal caverns and then aids them in attempting to effect the children's escape from their "prison".

During the highly-charged climax we see King attempt to flee the encircling helicopters overhead who seek to preserve the coastal retreat and its secrecy, eventually forcing King to crash his car off the pier and into the murky depths of the ocean.

Wells and Joan escape via the relative sanctuary of his boat as they are glimpsed sailing unchallenged out to sea, although both are left infected with the radiation levels which remain a bi-product of the children's enforced captivity.

The most chilling moments however, are reserved for Freya's hapless artist, who, having learned the truth behind Bernard's "scientific" experiment, vociferously voices her anger only to be arbitrarily executed in a hail of bullets fired by the calculating Bernard, Freya appropriately dying next to her cliff-top statues as she refuses to keep his secret.

As the final shots of the rugged coastline and all-enveloping ocean covers the screen, we hear the children's anguished cries: "Someone help us, please help us" in desperation as their nightmare is left to continue unabated.

It is during these climactic scenes that Bernard's misguided theories are expanded upon: "I live with one fact. A power has been released that will melt these shores," he claims as nuclear armageddon approaches.

He continues that: "To survive the destruction that is inevitably coming, we need a new kind of man," which is where his child proteges are integrated into his plans.

In his emotional sparring with Freya he announces that: "Every civilised nation is searching, searching for the key to survival which we have found".

Her powerful invective is: "What earth Bernard? What earth will you leave them? After all that man has made and still has to make. Is this the extent of your dream? To set nine ice-cold children free into the ashes of the universe?".

It is these germane words which serve to underline the futility of Bernard's mistaken quest for creating the ultimate superhuman, with his own rampant ego allowing him to cast himself in the role of creator – effectively god.

At one stage during the film he even calls out to "his" children that "I love you", but any genuine emotional impact is dissipated by the fact that he chooses to interact, not face to face, but only remotely with them and therefore, unemotionally attached via the TV monitor. This is a fact not lost on the isolated offspring who respond in unison: "You don't, you don't". They may not all fully understand their exact circumstances and the unusual predicament they find themselves in, but as children they *do* understand and recognise genuine and unconditional love when they see it, and they *don't* see it here.

Reed's measured performance here sees him move from anti-social to social in characterisation amidst the convoluted nuances at work within his psyche, and it is also interesting to see him as the counterpoint in many ways to Knox's scientist Bernard – both being "leaders" in their own very different circles before they converge during the final conflict. Otherwise, in some respects, Reed's role is rather thinly sketched – "All I was doing was riding around on motorcycles," he later said flippantly of his character here. Yet the young actor not only conveys his trademark brand of simmering menace, but successfully recreates the duality he had evinced so powerfully in Terence Fisher's **Curse Of The Werewolf**.

In the final analysis, Losey's well-developed intellectual motifs are perhaps at the expense of any greater immediacy in the plot dynamics – the action scenes occur, but not with the same degree of conviction present in the diametrically opposed views espoused by Bernard and Freya, for example. This reticence towards visceral drama on Losey's part precluded any further collaborations with Hammer, which studio head Michael Carreras was all to ready to foster, but floundered on Losey's negative response to the "overt violence" which he found contained in all the Hammer scripts he was sent.

Losey's own preferred working title was indeed "The Brink", which perhaps looked prophetic in terms of world events by the time of the Cuban missile crisis soon after the film's release, whilst it was actually filmed against the global backdrop of the Berlin Wall being constructed and with the Cold War tensions increasing after the shooting down of a U2 spy plane.

Indeed, it was these such political ramifications which played a large part in the film's delayed release in the States (by some 2 years in fact), with it eventually slipping through the net forming the lower half of a double bill with **Maniac** in 1963.

The renaissance of art and the subsequent reproach of science remains Losey's most striking achievement within this film, an audacious conceit for such avowedly sci-fi orientated subject matter and indeed, its intended audience.

I'LL NEVER FORGET
WHAT'S'IS NAME

"I'm going to find an honest job"
—Andrew Quint (Oliver Reed)

"Silly boy. There aren't any"
—Jonathan Lute (Orson Welles)

There's a kind of delicious irony to Reed's collaboration here with director Michael Winner – whom he also worked with on **The System** (1966), **The Jokers** (1967) and **Hannibal Brooks** (1969) and, more latterly, in one of the last films before his death, **Parting Shots** (1998) – because Reed has also worked with the equally ubiquitous Ken Russell on the likes of **Women In Love** (1969) and **The Devils** (1971), with all three men being very much grouped together as the *enfants terribles* of British cinema throughout their careers.

Whether in each or all cases this *enfant terrible* sobriquet is warranted is highly debateable, but let's get one thing straight immediately – controversial, opinionated and boorish though Winner may be, he can, repeat *can*, direct and make watchable films. The litany of violence and sexual degradation he leaves in his wake with **Death Wish** (1974), **The Sentinel** (1977) and **Dirty Weekend** (1993) may be inauspicious but whichever way you cut it, **I'll Never Forget What's'is Name** (1967) is a vibrant, captivating work of real repute.

From the very opening moments as we are instantly inveigled into the "swinging sixties" via the electric, snazzy soundtrack music and advertising executive Andrew Quint (Oliver Reed) is glimpsed joining the sprawling swathes of London commuters, immaculately clad in a suit but carrying an axe (!) casually over one shoulder, we know that we are in for a compelling viewing experience.

Reed's portrayal of Quint, an idealist not solely motivated by money like the rest of the commuter rat-race, is far removed from his customary hellraiser roles and the entire film engenders an ironic tone from both his (and others') ultimately futile pursuit of happiness.

The surreal image of Quint brandishing the axe during the opening scenes is soon explained as he breezes into his agency office and summarily begins to demolish his desk, each swinging axe blow a strike for freedom in his eyes.

His mercurial boss, Jonathan Lute (Orson Welles) doesn't appreciate Quint's dramatic gesture of resignation... "You're so ridiculously good at your job," he observes, even claiming that "You verge on genius".

Such fulsome praise and eulogising fails to impress Quint however, who manages to encapsulate his own altruistic idealism into one succinct reply: "I don't like the work. It's deceitful, superficial and self-indulgent".

As Quint retreats to his shared flat, contemplating his new career as assistant editor of his old friend Nicholas' (Norman Rodway) literary magazine, his fellow lodger Walter (Edward Fox) poignantly remarks: "So, you're a well dressed beatnik. Half-way out of society, half-way in".

The rapid pacing complements perfectly Quint's tangled private life, whose collateral includes his estranged wife Louise (Wendy Craig) and child, plus a veritable harem of mistresses including Josie (Marianne Faithfull) and Susannah (Lyn Ashley), and now the secretary with his new firm, Georgina (Carol White), whose alluring looks also conceal an active intellect.

When she questions Quint as to why he has quit his well-paid job he replies: "I was trying to get away from the rat race," and he explains his failed marriage thus: "I'm an unsuitable candidate for matrimony".

More personal revelations of even more importance are uncovered when Quint takes Georgina to his old school reunion night. Aside from Michael Horden's hilarious cameo as the school's forgetful headteacher, events take a rather more sinister turn as the school's old bully, Maccabe (Harvey Hall), decides to mercilessly hunt down one unfortunate ex-pupil, Eldritch (Roland Curram), as if a dog, in an attempt to recapture the "halcyon" days of his former thuggery. After Maccabe and his cronies have pursued the frightened man through the nearby woods and across the lake, Quint then intervenes showing commendable courage to help Eldritch escape.

Heavily outnumbered, Quint takes a brutal beating under the horrified gaze of Georgina. A tinted dream/nightmare sequence then shows a young Quint at school being berated by the chaplain (Frank Finlay) for his antipathy towards sports – "The man who is not interested in sport, is not interested in living with other people" – before the dazed Quint then awakes to find himself on Georgina's houseboat the next morning.

An early visit from his former boss Lute fails to offer either man much succour as Quint rejects the offer of taking his old job back, whilst Lute nearly chokes on the breakfast cereal he tastes – ironically a product his own firm has been promoting – showing that advertising really does leave a bad taste in the mouth after all!

The semantics of advertising and promotion rear their ugly head again as this time Quint debates with his new employer – "You know, we're going to have to change the image of the magazine Nicholas". Nicholas' rather patronising reply explains that: "I don't expect you to understand Andrew, but images are for the world of advertising. Literature doesn't have images." Literature may not have images per se but the intrinsic link in selling literature through the use of powerful images (witness any glossy magazine), is completely lost on the blinkered Nicholas.

Whilst all may not be entirely rosy at work, Quint's relationship with Georgina at least continues to flourish – "You're such a romantic aren't you. You've made the gesture that other people dream about and look where you've ended up," she announces ironically as she sits with Quint in the local launderette as he vacantly watches his washing spinning around.

Whilst Georgina's views emanate from her affection for Quint, the same cannot be said for his old squeeze Susannah, filming a commercial in a swimming pool, who taunts the on-looking Quint over his new "sad life" and not quite being able to give up anything. Quint's short-fuse is clear for all to see as he instinctively dives into the pool, having to be restrained from almost strangling the vitriolic Susannah.

His ultra-complicated personal life and assorted affairs continually contrive to hamper Quint in his seemingly genuine quest for Georgina – perhaps in her he has finally found his true soul mate – or is she merely destined to be yet another notch on the bedpost?

Quint's inpromptu liaison with his wife, ending up with the two of them in bed, doesn't serve to clarify his feelings; "Do you want a divorce?" he asks with "No, not tonight," being the inconclusive reply.

When Quint later takes Georgina with him to Cambridge in order to interview a prospective writer for the magazine, she is forced to reprimand him for his failed relationships: "Oh Andrew, shut up. Don't you think of anyone else but you?"

It is an event of epoch-making proportions however, which then strikes not just Quint, but has other far-reaching ramifications. He arrives at work as normal only to discover that Nicholas, under the shrewish guidance of his wife Carla (Ann Lynn), has arbitrarily sold their shares in the magazine to a publishing company located upstairs in the same building. Bitter and betrayed, Quint races upstairs to interrogate his new employer – only to stumble upon the surreal scene of an office decorated in Far-Eastern style decor and with Lute sat decadently playing with a scalextric set!

As Quint struggles to fight back his anger and recover from the shock, Lute philosophises that: "Waste" is going to be the big product of the twentieth century – a remark which brings satire to new heights given his own involvement in the vacuous advertising industry and Nicholas' equally vapid magazine, whose sales have long since plummeted.

"Waste, waste, waste for poetry that is no longer read and

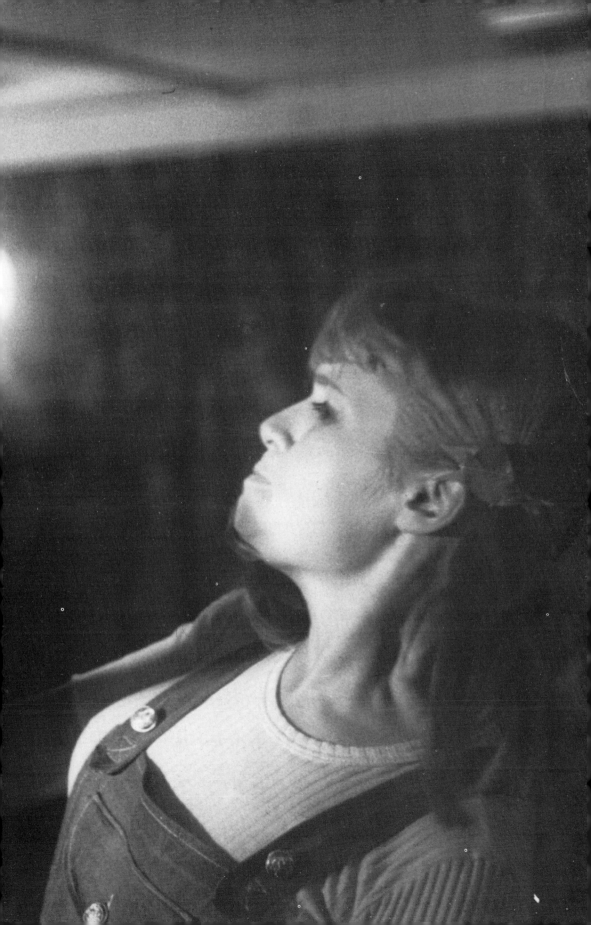

paintings that are no longer looked at, and the outer wrappings of processed cheese..." Lute rants, "...all standing on a great mountain of garbage". He finishes pointedly to Quint that: "It's up to you and me to see that we're standing on it and not under it".

So, the futility of Quint's attempts to leave the "rat-race" is fully established here as, having made the break from Lute and the world he represents, he still remains under his control after the circular chain of events has unfurled.

As the emotionally-battered Quint seeks to lick his wounds he confides to Georgina that he will "Make a bloody commercial that tells the truth – see if he gets an award for that", alluding to Lute's meritocratic pursuit of a "coveted" advertising industry award.

The symbolism of Quint and Georgina finally consummating their burgeoning relationship on the back of Quint's germane words is not lost. For once, Quint is being honest both in his actions *and* his words.

With his plans now formulated, Quint sets about taking full control over the shooting of the new commercial he is working on for Lute – his idealism and altruistic mentality at odds with the prolific materialism of Nicholas and Carla, who we discover merely sold off their shares (and their souls?) in pursuit of a washing machine and a new sports car.

It is this blatant, crass symbol of rampant materialism, the sports car, which ultimately proves fatal for both Nicholas and Georgina as, having basically forced Georgina to take a ride with him despite his drunken state, he proceeds to crash the car

– escaping himself but leaving Georgina trapped inside as the car explodes into flames.

The absolute nadir of human insensitivity is then revealed when Nicholas stumbles onto the houseboat to inform the now distraught Quint of Georgina's tragic death; "The car's completely wrecked," he stammers in words of uncaring ineptitude as Quint instinctively punches him before then vomiting over the side of the boat.

His life now ruined, his only meaningful contribution left is to vent his anger on the hypocrisy and superficiality of the advertising world during the bravura closing scenes.

As the industry "dignitaries", including the expectant Lute, converge on the awards ceremony, so does Quint's new commercial begin to unspool before them. Advertising the Hamayasha Super 8mm Camera, bikini-clad girls caress the product, promising that it will capture "your loved ones" and "those golden days with the family" – expertly intercut with scenes Quint has shot of him arguing with his wife. The gushing commentary continues: "Preserves forever those you have known" again, ironically intercut with a car crashing (symbolic of Georgina's death) and "capture those childhood memories that mean so much" – again juxtaposed with the unhappy schoolboy Quint being lambasted by his teacher for not playing sport.

Quint's final piece de resistance is his intercutting of Lute's words that "In the twentieth century the main product of all human endeavours will be waste" with footage of Quint operating a mechanical digger to scoop up literally hundreds of the Hamayasha cameras being advertised and then dumping them in a giant waste skip.

Commercial over, we then jump to Quint being presented with the award – "It's not for me Hugh, it's for the whole industry" being his ironic, not to mention, prophetic words. The evening ends in a brutal brawl between Quint and Maccabe, with the latter finally knocked unconscious into an ornamental fountain.

The next morning sees Quint walking along the Thames, throwing his award off a bridge and into the murky waters below and being reunited (?) with his wife – now talking of joining an advertising competitor, Dallafield, as they drive off together into the sprawling commuter mass that is London.

Oliver Reed's sensitive performance, aided capably by Carol White's inveigling portrayal of Georgina, gives us credible characters that we can both sympathise with and genuinely care about. Georgina's pathos-inducing death is very much a blow to our hearts as much as it is to Quint. Quint's continual quest for "true" love and to do something because he wants to do it, for artistic or aesthetic values rather than monetary values, also strikes a chord as being a worthwhile if perhaps unattainable goal.

Quint's throwaway comment at one stage on quitting his job that: "I never really saw the money anyway, it came in and went out, if I felt like being successful I'd go and buy a new shirt" perfectly encapsulates his non-materialistic approach to life. He is not driven or influenced by money, or the artificial trappings which it brings, merely by his ultimately forlorn hope of achieving personal happiness.

Winner keeps the action moving at a suitably kinetic pace whilst skilfully (and surprisingly) not sacrificing character subtleties and emotional detail in the process. His memorable portrayal of key, symbolic events, be they the public school reunion, the satirical awards ceremony or the pointless death of Georgina, are all superbly rendered and absolutely fundamental to the success of the film.

Given all the vibrancy and creative talent on display, the only sobering element is the conclusion, where seemingly all attempts to break the deadening propriety of the work ethic in society are suggested to be futile.

Of incidental interest here is also Josie's vitriolic outpouring to Quint at one stage to "Get out of here, you fucking bastard!" – vying with Joseph Strick's **Ulysses** (1967) as the first use of the "f" word on the big screen, plus one scene between Quint and Georgina which implies oral sex, which led to the American MPAA denying the film its seal of approval, leading to the distributors Universal, instead distributing the film via a subsidiary route, not signed to the MPAA. Along with a similar scene in Albert Finney's **Charlie Bubbles** (1968), this helped to see the end of the then in-place Production Code and its replacement with the ratings system currently used in the States.

Whilst retaining elements of his growing public persona as both womaniser and brawler in the character of Quint, Oliver Reed turns in a performance which suggests new depths as an actor. Although, ultimately, Reed's compelling performances in Ken Russell's **Women In Love** and **The Devils** overshadow even his excellent efforts here, it is hard to think of a finer movie moment for Winner, eclipsing his other work with a confident display of style, depth and vision not generally associated with his oeuvre.

Even the film's jokey, irreverent title, perfectly complements the action which unfolds as each character, especially Quint, tries to carve out their own indelible impression upon the landscape of humanity – ultimately a failure, but a valiant failure – at least in the case of Quint.

WOMEN IN LOVE

"You know, I always believe in love. True love.
But where do you find it nowadays?"
—Gerald Crich (Oliver Reed)

Just as the much-maligned Michael Winner proved he could cut the directorial mustard with the engaging **I'll Never Forget What's'is Name**, so here, does the similarly chastised Ken Russell direct with some aplomb, this fine 1969 adaptation of D H Lawrence's novel *Women In Love*. Russell had previously directed Reed in his two television films *The Debussy Film* and *Dante's Inferno*, offering him a lifeline from potential type-casting as a glowering thug, and the actor's role in **Women In Love** finally gave him the chance to shine as an actor.

The story, set in the 1920's north of England, centres on two parallel love affairs which unfold between Rupert Birkin (Alan Bates) and Ursula Brangwen (Jennie Linden) and also Gerald Crich (Oliver Reed) and Ursula's sister, Gudrun (Glenda Jackson). It is this singular love "quadrangle" which proves **Women In Love**'s main axis as we are gradually introduced to the diverse personalities involved. Reed's Gerald, resplendent in top hat and tails and also fretting that his sister Laura (Sharon Gurney) will be late for her wedding; "Something unconventional will do that family good," observes one onlooker, but for Gerald this is too intolerable – "What a spectacle," he complains, continuing with his personal ethos that you "Do something proper or don't do something at all".

We next see Gerald swimming "properly", i.e. as naked as nature intended, to the amusement of Ursula and Gudrun – "He's got go anyhow," Ursula remarks; "Oh, he's got go, but

the important thing is where does his go, go to," replies Gudrun.

A major part of Gerald's "go" is directed towards the local mineworks which he owns and runs, though not with the universal support of his employees; as Ursula points out, he is "making all kind of latest improvements – they hate him for it".

Our first major initiation into the rather hedonistic world of school inspector Rupert, is humorously during a picnic where he "treats" his captivated audience to a Freudian discourse by likening the properties of a fig to the female sex organs, whilst his vacuous relationship with his present "date", Hermione (Eleanor Bron), is signposted as a once fruitful offering which has now over-ripened.

While Rupert is concerned with more decadent pursuits and fanciful philosophies, we see Gerald as being more firmly rooted in the harsh realities of the present day, demanding a ruthless streak which he is more than capable of obliging, as we see him with blackened face, entering the pit in order to dismiss those miners he deems are not working hard enough, as well as being castigated for stopping the benevolent supply of "widow's coal" allocated to miner's widows, previously instigated by Gerald's father Thomas (Alan Webb).

"They hate you," his father divulges to Gerald when debating the disaffected work force, with "I give them a fair salary, if they can do the work," being Gerald's riposte. He continues unabated that: "The firm's not the charitable institution that you seem to think it is father".

Despite this perceived show of recalcitrance, coupled with his brutalising horse-riding technique – repeatedly digging his spurs into his mare in front of a shocked Gudrun – Gerald does manage to, for once, make the right impression when he saves Gudrun from an unsavoury pub brawl and from one employee's lecherous advances and propositioning of her.

The relationship further blossoms when Gudrun and Ursula are next invited to the Crich's family party held in their spacious mansion grounds. Having boated down the adjacent river, we are then treated to the surreal sight of Gudrun dancing in front of a field of bulls, before she then rushes towards the bemused animals to chase them away.

Upon witnessing this bizarre scene, Gerald rebukes her: "Why are you behaving in this impossible, ridiculous fashion?" as

Gudrun continues cavorting in front of him now, arching her shoulders theatrically like a ballet dancer, complete with ivory-white dress and tights to reinforce the image.

We then journey into the very heart of the subject matter – the eternal quest for "true love", if such an ideal does indeed exist – the sudden death of Laura and her husband, drowned in the river, provoking the prophetic remark from Gerald to Gudrun: "That's one thing about our family you know. Once something goes wrong it can never be put right. Not with us".

Almost simultaneously as Gerald is casting himself as if some doomed figure from Greek Tragedy, Rupert is similarly bearing his soul to Ursula thus: "Oh, I love you right enough. I just want it to be something else". The contrast between Gerald and Rupert is drawn in that whilst Gerald is damned for never truly grasping the object of his desires, likewise Rupert is damned for never being satisfied with what he has got, having reached his goal.

As Hermione's profound statement that: "Perhaps it is better to die than to live mechanically. Repetition after repetition," withers slowly on the vine, we can glimpse a greater emotional bond forming, not between the men and their partners, but between Rupert and Gerald themselves, highlighted by their "infamous" naked wrestling scene.

With a blazing fire roaring in the background, the intimate lighting and relaxed atmosphere creates a genuine warmth in which both men strip bear their souls, both emotionally and physically.

"My god, I've just reached the conclusion that nothing mattered

in the world except somebody to take the edge off one's being alone. The right somebody," Gerald reveals to Rupert. "Meaning a woman I suppose?" being Rupert's ambiguous response.

Gerald's rejoinder is thus: "Yes, of course. Failing that, an amusing man". He continues; "You know, I've got the feeling that if I don't watch myself I might do something silly". Having wrestled mentally with the perennial mystery of love and its elusiveness, they then literally wrestle with each other, throwing one another to the ground and locked in wrestling embraces as if a pair of carefree lovers.

As their sweating torsos recuperate from their playful activities, the physically superior Gerald asks pointedly: "Was it too much for you?" before Rupert, pondering and espousing even further his own philosophies to Gerald in response, proffers that: "We are mentally and spiritually close, therefore we should be physically close. It's more complete".

As if to reinforce their new-found bond, call it bloodbrothers or soul mates if you will, Gerald addresses the central issue: "You know, I always believe in love. True love. But where do you find it nowadays?"

Just as Gerald is mentally and spiritually "consummating" his relationship with Rupert, so too does he finally consummate his physical relationship with Gudrun – immediately after the death of his father and his mother's criticism of him for being too self-important, still ringing in his ears.

Striking deep into the heart of the issue is Ursula's protestation that Rupert – "tripping off into the beyond" – seeks both a physical wife and a spiritual wife, the increasing suggestion becoming that whilst Ursula fulfils the former role, perhaps it is Gerald who fulfils the latter.

The envisaged clean break from such troublesome realities as both couples take off to the Swiss mountains on holiday, fails to materialise and gradually only serves to drive a wedge between Gudrun and Gerald, and bring Gerald and Rupert closer together.

As Gerald confides in Rupert: "Do you know what it is to suffer when you're with a woman? It tears you like silk. And each bit and stroke burns. Hot."

With each new hour seemingly accelerating this burning process, Gudrun admonishes Gerald: "You have so little grace. So little finesse," with his heart-felt response being that: "You break me and waste me and it is horrible to me".

Even their subsequent frenzied "lovemaking" corrupts the very word – more akin to rape, their actions borne out of frustration and rage on Gerald's part whilst Gudrun's cold, clinical cynicism parallels the icy milieu they now inhabit.

Her chill demeanour is now perfectly encapsulated in her liaison with a local lounge (or ski slope) lizard, the effeminate Loerke (Vladek Sheybal); they play decadent games together, he, applying make-up to her face as she oozes: "Cleopatra must have been (the) hardest. She reaped the essential from a man. She harvested the ultimate sensation and then threw away the husk".

Given Gudrun's recent actions, these sentiments reveal yet more about her personality and life (love) ethos, culminating with her final acidic remarks to Gerald that: "You're so limited. You're a dead end. You cannot love".

Having punched Loerke and nearly strangled Gudrun in his unsurprising anger, Gerald then stumbles inconsolably away, a broken man, faltering in the thick snow and isolated mountains, finally collapsing in a semi-foetal position in the enveloping snow, where he will soon freeze to death.

The aching contrast in reactions to his death – Gudrun sets off for Dresden (in pursuit of the egregious Loerke), whilst Rupert lies crying over the sight of his friend's now frozen body, indicates who had the most love for Gerald.

Rupert pours out his torment to Ursula: "You are enough for me as far as a woman is concerned. You are all women to me. But I wanted a man friend, as eternal. As you and I are eternal," he explains.

"You can't have two kinds of love. Why should you?" Ursula complains; "It's impossible," she pleads. "I don't believe that," are Rupert's prophetic words as the strident music score signals the end of the film and yet, true to the original novel, leaves the question of love and all the differing philosophies surrounding it, unresolved.

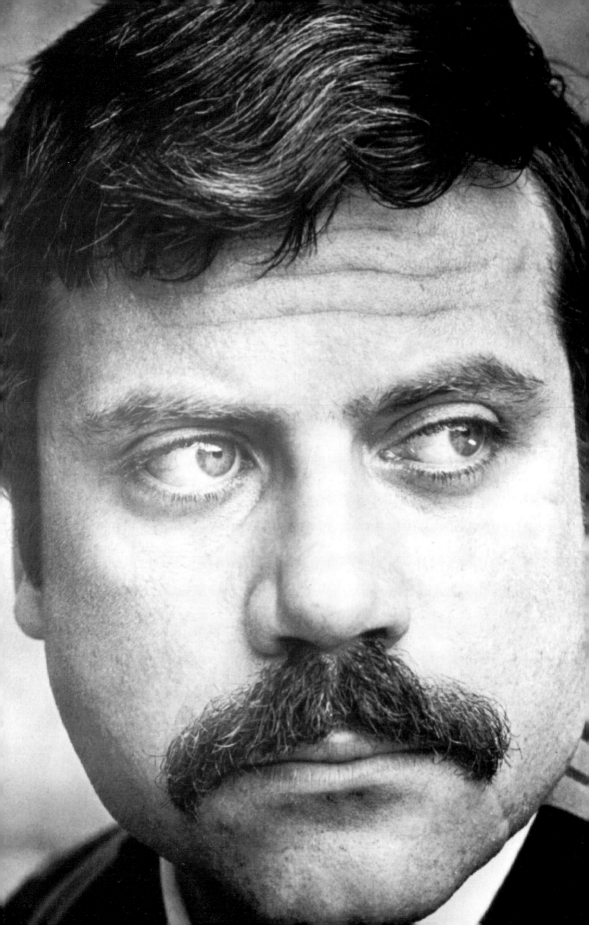

Ultimately, **Women In Love** offers us a detailed and fascinating analysis as to the complexity of both love, in its multifarious forms, and human relationships with certain characteristics, nuances and subtleties of the human psyche which we can all recognise and empathise with.

The diverse characters the action revolves around, from the manipulative Gudrun who sees relationships in terms of what she can get out of them, to the naive but engaging Ursula who sees love as a pure and simple thing – an eternal bond between man and wife – from Gerald's strong but boarish businessman to Rupert's more aloof believer in multifaceted forms of love, enable us to fully explore the tempestuous relationships therein, in what has been dubbed "a masterful examination of sexual domination and repression".

With Reed, Bates and Linden perhaps unfortunate to have been overlooked, Jackson at least did win her first Oscar for her performance as Gudrun and later followed this up by starring as the *mother* of her character here in Russell's prequel, **The Rainbow** (1989).

Russell himself was deservedly Oscar-nominated for his capable handling of the material, which renders memorable visual and emotional scenes, ably complimented by writer Larry Kramer's concise screenplay (also Oscar-nominated), which successfully dramatises Lawrence's work for the big screen, but without diluting it, remaining less convoluted than its source novel without sacrificing any of the characterisation integral to its success.

Given the way that Jackson's ever-burgeoning sexuality, parodied here as nymphomania, and her incisive intellect which subsides in favour of mere bitchiness here is portrayed, it was perhaps of no real surprise when Russell picked up the baton again in casting the similar Vanessa Redgrave as the sexually frustrated and hysterical Sister Jeanne alongside Reed's Grandier in **The Devils** (1971).

Oliver Reed gained so much attention for the nude wrestling scene that it probably undermined his performance, which was probably his best to date. He recalls that they were even reviled as "pornographers" in Italy, where the film was banned.

THE DEVILS

"I have a great need to be united with God"
—Father Urbain Grandier (Oliver Reed .

This compelling, invigorating and often hysterical witch's brew of history, surrealism, black comedy and human frailty forms a potent concoction, mixed as it is from Whiting's play *The Devils* and Aldous Huxley's book *The Devils Of Loudon*, and brought to the boil by the eccentric Ken Russell's wildly imaginative direction (aided by Derek Jarman's stunning set designs) to form **The Devils** (1971).

After the controversy whipped up by Russell and Oliver Reed by the nude wrestling scene in their previous collaboration **Women In Love, The Devils** went one step further with its "blasphemous" visions of religious corruption, torture and sexual mania.

The fiery locale is 17th century France, a fermenting mass of political and religious debate with the principal division being between the King, Louis XIII (Graham Armitage), who seeks to preserve both the regal and regional government of pre-renaissance France – a view widely supported by Oliver Reed's priest, Grandier – and the power-hungry forces marshalled by Cardinal Richelieu (Christopher Logue) who ultimately seek to enforce one view, one doctrine, upon a whole nation in a dictatorial structure of centralised government.

As Grandier controls the city of Loudon, reinforced by the imposing walls and battlements which safeguard its autonomy, he is immediately propelled into a fatal collision course with Richelieu, whose response is to falsely accuse Grandier of being

a heretic in order to discredit him and so destroy him, and ultimately Loudon.

Utilising the frenzied "testimony" of the crippled, Grandier-obsessed Mother Superior, Sister Jeanne (Vanessa Redgrave), the sadistic methods of witchfinder general Father Barre (Michael Gothard) and the insidious political scheming of Baron De Laubardemont (Dudley Sutton), an orchestrated campaign to sully Grandier is set in motion with fatal consequences for both the priest, for France and for democracy as a whole.

Richelieu's corrupt intentions are evidenced during the film's opening scene as he sits impassively watching the King's starring role in a palace play before venturing; "A most original conception your majesty. The birth of Venus. I pray that *I* may assist *you* in the birth of a new France, where church and state are one," a scene which artfully cuts into the spiralling face of a gnarled skeleton, left spinning on an elevated wheel as Richelieu's forces march in the direction of Loudon.

Grandier, with unkempt black hair and moustache, clad in gold and black robes, then addresses his "flock", preaching in front of white church walls and glass windows which tower behind him and up into the sky and seemingly, infinity. "The religious wars are over. Catholic no longer fights with Protestant. We have survived," he preaches to the expectant crowd below.

A rapid cut then catapults us into the thriving mass and hysterical nuns in the crowd, all struggling to view the ornate funeral procession for Loudon's late governor, Saint Mart, whose dying breaths bequeathed the city's control to Grandier.

As Grandier is shown leading the ensemble, one female

onlooker stares at him and gushes: "He's the most beautiful man in the world," with other similarly obsessed women joining the chorus – "Grandier can have me anywhere, even on the holy order itself" and "Now there's a man well worth going to hell for" reinforcing the consensus.

Sister Jeanne's own sexual frustration at glimpsing the object of her desires, Grandier, then manifests itself in the form of a feverish dream as she imagines the Christ-like Grandier walking across water, literally parting the waves, towards her, a sea of black flags held aloft contrasting vividly with her own flowing red hair. The dream abruptly shatters into a nightmare however, as the rising wind exposes her "beauty" to Grandier as her ungainly hunchbacked frame is revealed.

Her dreams of sexual union with Grandier give way to the reality of the priest's sexual tryst with the unfortunate Philippa (Georgina Hale), who is now pregnant with Grandier's "holy" seed – a curious bi-product of her intended Latin lessons with her religious tutor!

"You must learn to bear your cross with Christian fortitude," Grandier responds sanctimoniously to her, continuing by reminding her to: "Remember, we laughed as we roused the animal and now its devoured us," as he seeks to justify their illicit affair. Grandier then begins to expand on his own personal philosophy upon the merits of the flesh and the vulnerability it also brings: "The body can transcend its purpose. It can become a thing of such purity that it can be worshipped to the limits of the imagination. Everything is allowed. All is right. And such perfection leads to an understanding of this hideous state of existence. But what is it now? An egg. A thing of loneliness, weariness, sickness," he surmises.

Grandier then rubs salt into an increasingly emotional wound by callously disregarding Philippa and advising her to tell her father, Tricant (John Woodvine) and to try and find a "good" man – "They exist," he says disparagingly.

"Hold my hand. It's like touching the dead isn't it?" he enquires of her as he then retreats from her pleas for help. Grandier's subsequent spat with Tricant results in impasse – "I'll see you in hell," the enraged parent shouts; "Walking on a living pavement of aborted bastards no doubt," being Grandier's ironic riposte.

As Grandier moves on to a new relationship with Madeleine (Gemma Jones), his sexual proclivities may not exactly engender audience empathy, but his humane spirit and fortitude in other areas certainly does.

In a portentous scene, he castigates the arcane "torture" methods meted out to a suspected witch, reprimanding her assailants for using potions, powdered mistletoe, poppies, black cherries, leeches and even a crocodile (!), which Grandier summarily throws into a fire.

"You stand on the threshold of everlasting life. I envy you," are Grandier's parting words to the suffering victim as she expires – prophetic words as he too, will soon be the victim of medieval torture methods and be preparing for the life eternal.

At least Grandier recognises his own frailties, especially his weakness of and for the flesh, as he confides to a colleague Mignon (Murray Melvin) as he administers the last rites to plague victims, surrounded by a wall of bleach white corpses, and explains his need to meet his maker, requiring his various women and whores to turn upon him, casting him as a doomed figure.

Grandier's inevitable demise is also predicted in another of Sister Jeanne's fever dreams as she again visualises Grandier as Christ, wearing the Crown of Thorns and stepping down from the cross and kissing her, whilst Grandier's words of justification to Madeleine after they consummate their partnership are: "I take the words of our creator as gospel. It is not good for man to be alone".

The plans to usurp Grandier then gather apace as we see

Grandier arguing with the Catholic-led soldiers of Baron De Laubardemont, who begin to attack the city walls and battlements of Loudon. "Should one more stone be taken from these city walls, you will be dead before it touches the ground," Grandier promises the now encircled Baron.

With the enemy now retreating Grandier has won the battle but not the war, as Richelieu is shown attempting to persuade the King to dismantle the right to self-rule of those cities such as Loudon, whilst Grandier's later marriage to Madeleine in a ceremony he conducts himself, together with Sister Jeanne's hysterical evidence to Father Barre that Grandier is possessed by the devil, simultaneously sow the seeds of the hapless priest's eventual destruction.

It is this final third of the film where the draconian methods used to extract "confessions" come to the fore, as the lunacy of the "case" against Grandier is exposed and the futility of his impassioned defence, fully realised.

Frenzied scenes take place as Sister Jeanne is given a holy water enema (!) from a giant metal syringe, whilst the other similarly hysterical nuns are rounded up into a group and encouraged by the equally crazed Father Barre to purge themselves of their evil and lewd thoughts under his "guidance".

The height of this fabricated folly is all too easily apparent as the King himself visits the scene of debauchery, offering up a "relic" containing Christ's blood to monitor the effects for himself. As the lustful nuns all universally recant of their sins before him due to the "holy" powers of the artifact, the King simply reveals the relic to be an empty casket; so he instantly realises the deceit being perpetrated here. "Have fun," are his parting words to Sister Jeanne as she scuttles off to rejoin the orgy.

When Grandier also sees this hedonistic display for himself he admonishes them powerfully; "You have turned the house of the Lord into a circus. And its servants into clowns. You have seduced the people in order to destroy them. You have perverted the innocent".

As the grave implications of Sister Jeanne's fatuous claims begin to dawn on Grandier, he prepares himself mentally, if not physically for the ordeal to come. "I know what I have sown and I know what I must reap," he admits, going on to refute the accusations hurled at him of collusion with Satan, claiming he "cannot be a devil's boy as I don't have the humility".

Summarily arrested, Grandier is then systematically tortured in order to extract a false "confession" as Sister Jeanne – repulsed by her own duplicitous actions – simultaneously attempts to commit suicide by hanging herself from a tree.

The true horror of Grandier's predicament is amply illustrated as his torture takes place against the background trauma of seeing all his artefacts, offices and personal belongings being arbitrarily destroyed by the Baron's soldiers.

"Why don't you offer up your pain to god. You've lived by your senses, obviously you can die by them," the Baron callously taunts Grandier. His spiteful vitriol continues unabated: "You have one consolation. Hell will hold no surprises for you".

But as Grandier poignantly remarks during the start of his "trial": "You have totally perverted Christ's own teaching,"

alluding to the fact that it is seemingly only the "devil's word" which is now accepted as evidence, rather than the word (his word) of God. The heinous punishment meted out to Grandier is perpetrated in the name of God but its invidious construction betrays the work of the devil.

Bloodied but unbowed, Grandier continues his moving polemic against his centralist enemies, explaining that: "This new doctrine, especially invented for this occasion, is the work of men who are not concerned with the work of fact, or law, or with theology, but a political experiment to show how the will of *one* man can be pushed into destroying not only one man, or one city, but one nation".

Just and persuasive though his argument may be, Grandier realises that the amassed will of the political forces against him is far greater than his own, and he acknowledges in his words the even more ominous ramifications of this force, not just for him but for the entire country.

Stripped of his freedom, Grandier's dignity is next as he is shaved bald as he awaits the verdict of the court – the judges' pointed white caps appropriately evoking the image of those latterday fascist forces, the Ku Klux Klan; and when Grandier asks the Baron for a mirror, vanity is the last thing on his mind as he is forced to use his commode to glimpse his own reflection.

Duly sentenced to be burned alive, Grandier's emotive words fall on largely deaf ears. "My Lords, I *am* innocent of the charges and I am afraid. But I have the hope in my heart that before this day ends, almighty god will glance aside and let my suffering atone for my vain, disordered life. Amen".

Grandier continues, turning to the Baron, and explaining that: "I have no accomplices. These crimes are not my crimes. Please stop this foolishness. We both know why I have been brought to trial and why I have been found guilty".

Although now resigned to his fate and perhaps even welcoming the release from physical pain that his death will bring, Grandier's suffering is still not over as the Baron ruthlessly pursues a "confession" via his sadistic torturers, Grandier's legs being agonisingly broken and pulped by a battery of hammer blows.

Despite this savagery, Grandier still retains his sense of purpose and conscience, pointedly replying to Mignon's attempts to encourage his confession thus: "Do you believe in your conscience that a man should confess to crimes that he has not committed merely to ease his pain?".

Even at this eleventh hour, the Baron still pursues the political expediency his conniving mind craves, inviting Grandier to repent and embrace the church in order to prevent a "martyr's" death and so dissuade other "devil-possessed" warlocks from following the same path, whilst also placating the Catholic church; but Grandier refuses.

Grandier's harrowing execution follows, as he is forced to agonisingly crawl towards his own funeral pyre, hastily constructed in the main square, his bloodied stumps for feet, kicked callously by the leering Father Barre whilst the shrieking Mignon exhorts him to confess.

As Grandier is tied to the stake, his misery is nearing its completion as the pyre is lit and the orange flames begin to engulf him, his face rapidly turned into a blistering, charred mess by the intense heat.

Barely have the flames burned the last ounce of life from Grandier, than the Baron gives the signal for the city walls to be destroyed. Later, we see the pathos-inducing sight of Madeleine visiting the smouldering remains of the pyre, as the executioner is burying the debris that was once her husband – no Christian burial for Grandier being poignantly highlighted here.

As we see Madeleine walk along the now ruined city walls, we see the road ahead stretching into the distance, bleakly lined by elongated poles topped with wheels containing the (Protestant) corpses of those like Grandier who chose to fight against political tyranny. The jarring, dislocating cacophony of "music" which plays out the film, suitably encapsulates the nihilistic denouement.

The symbolic destruction of the city walls and of a country ravaged by the plague, all serve to underline the fact that the fundamental fabric of society is being eroded here, with personal freedom being sacrificed upon the altar of political indoctrination and expediency.

Providing most assuredly, Reed and Russell's finest hour, the blistering performances and daring subject matter of **The Devils** signalled genius to some, blasphemy to others, but the compelling hysteria of Redgrave's masterful turn, the humanity of Reed's beleaguered priest and the fanatical doctrines of Father Barre and the Baron, all herald an epic film, combining both style and substance. Reed later appeared in brief cameos in Russell's later **Mahler** and **Lisztomania**, before taking on a singing (!) role in Russell's version of The Who's rock opera

Tommy (alongside his hell-raising partner Keith Moon), but **The Devils** was to prove their last collaboration of note.

Although the *Aurum Encyclopedia Of Horror* spectacularly berated the film – "Russell indulges his predilection for camp imagery and his virulent contempt for women" – what is most salient in **The Devils** are Russell's attempts to champion personal autonomy, to harness the use of striking visual imagery, to condemn the manipulative ethos which underpins this kind of Machiavellian politics and to applaud the victory of supreme strength of spirit over convenient capitulation of the soul.

Grandier's bravery in the face of death creates a resonating image and the austere denouement is one which carves an indelible mark upon all who see it, elevating it to becoming one of the true icons of visionary cinema.

THE HUNTING PARTY

"You're gonna teach me to read – that's what you're here for."
—Frank Calder (Oliver Reed)

"He ain't what other people think he's like on the outside."
—Doc Harrison (Mitch Ryan) on Frank

As one of Olly's rare excursions into the western genre, **The Hunting Party** (1971) is a visceral and valedictory picture, aspiring to yet never quite achieving the dizzying heights of style and orchestrated violence embodied in the spaghetti western films which it so obviously apes.

That said, **The Hunting Party** remains an intriguing curiosity, both for the brutality it randomly displays and for the character subtleties which lie buried beneath the veneer of violence.

Director Don Medford, hitherto known for his (mainly) TV work as well as one of the engaging entries in the popular U.N.C.L.E. spy series – **To Trap A Spy** (1966) – filmed the action in Spain, as if to reinforce the spaghetti influence (as this is also where most of the Italian sagebrush opera's were filmed), and he succeeds in gathering a big-name cast in order to try and fill over some of the more blatant cracks in the tired plot.

So, we are introduced to the loathsome Brandt Ruger (Gene Hackman) – a sadistic cattle baron in Texas at the turn of the 19th century, his school-teacher wife, Melissa (Candice Bergen), and outlaw Frank Calder (Oliver Reed) and his gang of desperados.

Ruger's psychopathic tendencies are illustrated for all to see in the very opening scenes where we see Ruger making "hate" as opposed to "love" to his long-suffering wife – "Stop!" she pleads, with "Get dressed," being his curt reply.

Having established the physical abuse which he is happy to inflict upon Melissa, Ruger then adds mental cruelty to the "charge sheet" as he announces that he will be away on "business" travelling on his own private train for the next two weeks, callously rejecting Melissa's protestations that he stay with her.

The line of leering, grinning female faces that we then see pressed excitedly up against one of the train's windows, delineates Ruger's true "business" intent, which focuses squarely on the unique bordello carriage he insists on having.

As Ruger leaves we then see Frank and his gang menacingly encircle Melissa as she takes a class – Frank stooping suddenly from his horse in order to snatch Melissa and carry her away with him back to their camp. She is soon frightened by the palpable sexual tension she arouses in the gang – "We're just getting started," one says to her ominously – whereupon Frank intervenes, only for him to slap her down as she becomes hysterical: "I promise you. Ain't nobody gonna hurt you just as long as you do as you're told," he admonishes her.

The contrast here is then vividly drawn between Melissa, who is seemingly consigned to weeks of living rough on the arid, desert trail, whilst Ruger is shown revelling in the decadent lifestyle afforded to him by his wealth and the opulent train he travels on. We also see (significantly for later on) Ruger expanding on the attributes of the new rifle he now cradles – complete with telescopic sight and accurate for up to 800 yards.

Ruger exchanges one loaded "weapon" for another closer to home, as we see him unceremoniously commandeer one unfortunate girl to satiate his carnal lust – throwing her onto his luxurious bed with the romantic verse "Get undressed" rolling from his lips.

"Chinese are very special. I show you a good time," his oriental companion/victim generously offers, only for Ruger to rebuke her thus: "Oh, you're gonna show me a good time alright."

As we then cut back to the dishevelled, rather than decadent Melissa, her plight is rendered increasingly hopeless as Frank boasts: "It don't matter who's wife you are, 'cause there's nothing he can do about it."

When news reaches Ruger that Melissa has been effectively kidnapped – and who knows what else – by Frank and his feared gang who are now heading off north, Ruger immediately decides to pursue them aided by his own gang of outlaw cronies, utilising the new rifle in order to be able to pick off Frank's gang, one by one, and from a distance.

When the action switches to Melissa trying to escape the clutches of her captors, it is Frank who catches her and forces himself upon her. Their staccato encounter – he caresses her, she seeks to rebuff him, before their adulterous union is finally consummated – is both protracted and disquieting, blurring the boundaries between what exactly constitutes rape and what constitutes consent here. Their final embrace however, with Melissa kissing Frank more passionately suggests that already they have found the genuine affection for one another that appears to elude Melissa and Ruger.

Ruger's moral bankruptcy is reasserted when he shows nothing but contempt for his wife's well-being as he selfishly outlines the impact of her kidnapping on *him* as opposed to *her*: "He'll give her a kid and then we'll have a little outlaw bastard running around the house," he says of Frank.

He continues his tirade to the disbelieving Watt Nelson (Ronald Howard) – "What do you think he's gonna do with her, sing church hymns? He'll pass her around," he claims, continuing that "Who'd have a Virginia educated, butter wouldn't melt in her mouth wife used like a whore – and then I'll have to take her back pregnant, with a bastard and give him forty or fifty thousand dollars of my own money."

With her hair, formerly tied back in a regimented bun, now significantly free-flowing locks of shoulder-length blonde tresses, Melissa seems to be symbolically announcing her new sexual freedom and relationship with Frank. Frank says he isn't sorry for forcing himself upon her but Melissa flails at him (which he enjoys as it shows spirit), before then launching another unsuccessful escape bid – this time riding away on a horse.

"Who do you think you are, the Lord of Creation, driving at anybody not doing everything you want. You're nothing but an animal," she accuses Frank. Whilst he may betray his base, animal instincts repeatedly, Frank also harbours rather more sensitive ambitions as well, as he continues to beseech Melissa to teach him to read, with her steadfastly refusing thus far.

Eventually though, she does acquiesce in a humorous scene whereby Frank and his trusted colleague Doc Harrison (Mitch Ryan) are sat under a horse-drawn cart, drooling over Frank's bottle of juicy peaches, slurping the tasty fruit down their throats and teasing the hungry Melissa to join them – on condition that she agrees to teaching Frank to read.

Melissa enthusiastically dives in and devours the luscious fruit. "Do you know any of the alphabet?" she enquires of Frank, with "No" being his laughter-filled reply.

This brief display of frivolity is shortlived however, as we then cut to Ruger and his men spying on Frank through binoculars, before then lining up two of the outlaw's men between his rifle's crosshairs and pulling the trigger to signal their long-distance executions.

Although he repeatedly focuses on the bemused Frank in his crosshairs, Ruger neglects to pull the trigger on him, refrains from using such a cowardly, sniper's method (although he has no such compulsion about picking off Frank's men). In a balletic sequence of Peckinpah-styled slow-motion shootings, with arterial blood spraying across the screen, we see the majority of Frank's men gunned down in a desert watering hole.

When Ruger subsequently surveys the scene of his "triumph", he systematically removes the lifeless bodies from the bloodied water and lines them up along an adjacent bank as if they were human "trophies" for him to glory at. "Jesus Christ Brandt, stop it. They're not game we've bagged, they're seven men."

Ruger's atrocities and self-serving personality are counterpointed by Frank's far greater show of compassion – carefully tending to his now wounded companion Doc, by trying to extract a bullet from his stomach.

When Frank and Melissa subsequently seek refuge in a small border town, Frank is also on hand to comfort Melissa after she has been attacked by one of Frank's drunken gang – "I'm sorry," being his heartfelt apology to her as they climb into bed.

During the following hours when Ruger manages to catch up with one of Frank's wounded men, Ruger's hatred visibly increases as the nearly-dead outlaw claims of Melissa: "She's a hell of a woman," twisting the emotional knife by continuing that: "She likes it," – lovemaking, that is, with Frank – whereupon the enraged Ruger thrusts a dagger into the man's throat, so silencing him and his vocal cords.

As the rapidly tiring protagonists continue their game of cat and mouse, Watt implores Ruger to give up his deranged pursuit of his wife's captors. "Brandt, give it up. It doesn't make sense any more... you saw, let her go," he shouts in vain as Ruger sees Melissa deliberately choosing to be with Frank as opposed to him.

Again we see Frank tending to the wounded Doc, feeding him and wiping his fevered brow. This outer show of caring and loyalty contrasts vividly with the increasingly marginalised Ruger, whose own accomplices begin to desert him due to his psychopathic obsessions.

Frank then has to make an agonising decision when the rapidly failing Doc begs him to shoot him and end his misery. Walking away and subdued, Frank suddenly spins around and fires a round of bullets into his friend – a true mercy killing if ever there was one. Traumatised by having to kill his own best friend, Frank poignantly throws his gunbelt and rifle down – it is his final renunciation of violence.

With the denouement now fast approaching, it is only Frank and Melissa left alive now – still relentlessly pursued by Ruger across mountain streams and elevated forests which give way to the dry, blazing sun of the desert. As the intense heat gradually begins to take its toll, Frank and Melissa finally stagger and collapse exhausted onto the arid sand. Barely able now to open his eyes, Frank can vaguely glimpse the ominously approaching figure of Ruger, pacing through the shimmering heat haze that surrounds the sand like a halo. A solitary rifle shot however, signals that this will offer no sanctuary, as Frank falls to the ground, hit in the chest, then again and again. With the bullet-ridden Frank fighting tenaciously for his life, another shot sounds, only this time dealing Melissa a fatal wound in the stomach.

This final, nihilistic tableau sees Melissa's prone body lying in the sand, with Frank staring with bewilderment at his nemesis Ruger, who is now virtually upon him – Ruger eventually lying back in the sand exhausted having now looked upon a scene of total desolation, the empty wilderness he finds himself in mirroring perfectly his equally vacuous soul, devoid of any genuine *human* compassion for others.

This fatalistic ending – akin to Sergio Corbucci's **The Big Silence** (1968) – serves to underline the futility of wanton violence to the detriment of the human soul.

Whilst Hackman's turn as the sadistic, megalomaniacal cattle baron is utterly convincing, so too is Reed's loveable rogue – a far more complex character than first imagined, resorting to violence when necessary and yet never truly revelling in it. And

also showing commendable human spirit to care for those around him and to be able to shape his own personality and so change his outlook in his willingness to better himself, to learn to read and to ultimately, repudiate violence in favour of his pursuit of a more harmonious existence.

Bergen herself manages to invest her role with just the requisite amount of female vulnerability, hidden beneath a bold, forceful exterior as she seeks to escape her loveless marriage and find a more caring partner – Bergen had previously starred in Ralph Nelson's equally controversial western **Soldier Blue** (1970) – whilst composer Riz Ortolani's melancholic score – incessant strings motif coupled with dramatic, plaintive orchestration – obviously seeks to evoke the spellbinding, lyrical compositions of spaghetti western composer Ennio Morricone (as well as providing a trial run for Ortolani's equally moving score to Ruggero Deodato's highly controversial **Cannibal Holocaust** [1979]).

In an interview given at the time, Oliver Reed bemoaned the necessity of faking an American accent (as well as having to adopt the cowboy method of horse-riding – "you have to screw your arse into the saddle"), and this, coupled with his love for Broome Hall and English pub life, was enough to cement his decision to forgo the dubious delights of Hollywood.

SITTING TARGET

*"Why you're frightened of hitting somebody,
I'll never know Birdy"*
—Harry Lomart (Oliver Reed)

With the proliferation during the early 1970's of hard-hitting TV crime shows such as *Callan* and *The Sweeney*, and equally abrasive films such as **Villain** (1971) and **Get Carter** (1971), Douglas Hickox's **Sitting Target** (1972) proves to be equally adept at hitting the pressure points to the exclusion of any real semblance of human compassion.

In view of this, it is no surprise to be introduced to Reed's imprisoned Harry Lomart, barely biding his time "inside" before planning his prison breakout in order to gain revenge on his cheating wife Pat (Jill St. John). This revenge motif, the wanton violence which ensues and the palpable air of menace from the criminal underworld and of ex-cons polluting the mainly London milieu, all grasp inspiration from the aforementioned **Get Carter** (only here substitute London for Newcastle), with a similarly bleak and nihilistic conclusion in **Sitting Target** to boot.

Along with his best mate, Birdy (Ian McShane), Harry is seen playing out time as a clock pendulum swings during the opening shot of the film, before we then glimpse Harry busy exercising in his dark, shadowy cell. The throbbing bass soundtrack and strident orchestration – all pulsating and incessant – is *very* 1970's in sound as Harry continues to work out on the "parallel bars".

Gloom and despondency gives way momentarily to what transpires to be a false dawn for Harry as he meets his wife Pat during visiting hours – her first appearance there in the five months he has now been in prison. Harry's laconic reply as she praises the speed of the train which has transported her there is that "Well, everything moves quicker nowadays, except for in here of course".

His rather more searching question of "What you been doing?" however, elicits an unwelcome response as the reason for Pat's absence thus far is explained in that she has met someone else – "I want a divorce – I'm pregnant".

As far as dropping bombshells goes, this one is pretty well high up there on Harry's "resort to violence" list and sure enough, no sooner are the words uttered then his fist is plunging through the glass visitor's grille as he grabs hold of her neck and attempts to strangle her. With glass embedded in her neck and blood pouring out, the prison warders rush to her aid, simultaneously restraining the livid Harry using whatever force is necessary.

Next we see Harry, complete with straitjacket, housed in the bleak milieu of the solitary confinement wing, his mouth foaming and his previous screams of anguish echoing around him as if the haunting cries of a ghost.

Hickox utilises his visual flair in these scenes to the utmost, using low angle shots to accentuate the imposing height of the ever-looming prison cell walls, and there are repeated shots of gloomy, nebulous prison interiors complete with long shadows and sporadic shafts of light, often shot from behind stairs, grilles and bars. These rather stylised visuals help to reaffirm the inherent claustrophobia of the whole place and Harry's graphic spewing out of his first mouthful of prison tea renders the droplets silhouetted like a veritable breath of fetid air.

Against this build-up of almost utter despair and frustration, Harry's mounting anger, aided by his earlier fitness training, reaches its final outlet as he swivels himself up onto the ceiling of his cell, whereby he then launches himself at the helpless guards when they enter – the escape plan now in full swing at last.

With the help of his cell-mate and accomplice, Birdy, they overpower the guards and tie them up, though not before Birdy has emptied a brimming bowl of excrement and piss over one unfortunate guard. Other than this expression of anger, Birdy is reluctant to use violence, something which is anathema to Harry who is only too happy to cosh the guards with their own truncheons, pausing momentarily to enlist the assistance of fellow inmate, MacNeil (Freddie Jones) on their escape route.

The ensuing tension generated by the trio's daring pursuit of freedom remains one of **Sitting Target**'s most celebrated moments – Harry casually coshing unconscious another guard who helps facilitate their escape – "You need an alibi," being his flippant justification for the blow.

From here on in their journey to the "other side" becomes ever more precarious; scaling the towering prison walls and barbed-wire coils, negotiating a vicious guard dog in the sentry box, before utilising a grappling hook and line to engineer their own "death-slide" – the convicts praying that the patrolling warders below won't look up skywards to them.

With Birdy and MacNeil having slid to the comparative safety (if not freedom yet), of the outer prison wall, Harry's attempt

nearly ends in failure as the line breaks and he is forced to free-fall towards his comrades, before they all plunge simultaneously onto the canvas roof of a pre-arranged supplies van below which then transports to freedom.

This whole sequence is expertly-handled by Hickox and milks every last ounce of tension available – quickly dissipated through MacNeil's carnal desires as he makes rapid work of introducing himself to the willing female provided to satisfy his lascivious demands – "Two years celibacy is a bit too much for me – so if you'll excuse me," he motions to his companions.

His ardour knows no bounds as he gushes *"Lovely"* as he teases the girl's blouse open before burying his head between her breasts. Unconcerned by being only "second" in the queue, Birdy soon follows the same path but "I can do without," is Harry's cool, rejective response – all his energy focusing on revenge.

As Harry and Birdy then make their own way, separating from MacNeil the next day, it soon becomes clear that there are two distinct agendas at work here – Harry's and Birdy's. Whilst Birdy is merely content with surviving and trying to eke out a living by keeping a relatively low profile, Harry is consumed by the green-eyed monster – his one goal is visiting Pat and her new "squeeze" and taking out his own violent revenge.

Having located Pat in a high-rise flat, under the police protection of Inspector Milton (Edward Woodward), Harry, the red mist rapidly rising, soon sets about staking out the flat and battling with Milton on the towering balcony. Harry's subsequent escape leads to an imaginative chase scene where he runs for cover amongst a sea of washing lines and white sheets, narrowly avoiding the police motorcyclists who are in pursuit. When his well-aimed pistol shot strikes a petrol tank on one of the bikes, he effects his escape during the ensuing smoke and flames.

It is during Harry and Birdy's encounter with small-time crook (and police informer) Marty Gold (Frank Finlay) and his moll, Maureen (Jill Townsend), that Harry drops his guard and displays a rare moment of affection, when, in asking Maureen to run a bath for him, he merely cuddles her fur coat briefly before luxuriating in the cleansing bath like an excited child. At no stage does he seek to take advantage of the frightened and vulnerable girl, unlike his more base partner Birdy.

Having succeeded in silencing Marty – he is accidentally killed when he falls down the stairs – the duo fail in managing to extract any real money from him and a dramatic chain of events follows as first, Harry uses a gun armed with a telescopic sight in order to assassinate his wife (or so he believes), before Birdy then turns on him, kicking Harry unconscious down some railstation steps and escaping with what loot they have got. The gravity of Birdy's double-crossing and wicked deceit is revealed as he flees into a waiting car, driven by none other than... Pat.

Having discovered that the victim shot by Harry was in fact a policewoman guarding the flat, we then see the enraged Harry commandeer a land rover and give chase to the manipulative couple, who also reveal how Pat isn't really pregnant and that she trashed her own flat in order to be offered police protection in the first place.

Now that Harry has been safely snared in their web of lies, their only miscalculation is that he is still very much alive and breathing (down their necks) – "Bastard must be made out of concrete," is Birdy's withering remark on Harry's capacity for survival.

The ensuing kinetic car chase through the squalid London estates is again one of the film's major set-pieces, with Harry continually ramming his vehicle into the now terrorised accomplices. Eventually, Harry manages to launch their car through the air, spinning out of control and onto a railway line.

In a scene of high drama we see Pat lying dead inside the now shattered car whilst Birdy vainly runs off, only for Harry to shoot him dead in his tracks, appropriately holding onto the money he sought to steal, the notes spewing wastefully onto the ground.

As Harry spins round, silhouetted against an orange sky, he then returns to the remains of the car, planting a tender kiss on his dead wife's lips as flames suddenly explode and consume the car with Harry still inside.

The final sounds of rapidly approaching police sirens and the stark image of Milton blankly surveying the burning wreckage, only serve to reinforce the bleak denouement where greed and betrayal are more prevalent than humanity and integrity, ultimately leaving behind a trail of destruction with no winners.

In **Sitting Target** Oliver Reed is perfectly at ease portraying the single-minded, street-wise con Harry and yet, despite his repeated acts of brutality and violence, the revelatory conclusion strives to offer him up as at least an honest character emotionally – what you see is what you get (even if you don't particularly like it). Harry doesn't harbour the same feelings of insincerity or treachery so callously displayed by his wife and supposed "friend".

The admittedly negatory conclusion nonetheless reveals Harry's deep-seated tenderness, generally kept well hidden beneath his flailing fists, as the anger directs towards his wife betrays the fact that he does *care* passionately for her and doesn't want to lose her – but if he can't have her, then no one else can either.

He wears his heart on his sleeve for sure, but at least there is a heart there – something sorely lacking in both Pat and Birdy. Harry's earlier tenderness with Maureen and his rejection of an easy sexual encounter in the escape van, all indicate that for him, permanent, loving relationships are the only goal, not casual affairs for the sake of expediency.

Ultimately Harry is a wayward soul who one feels meets his almost inevitable end, once again lying alongside his wife – perhaps he will find more respect and reciprocal love with her in the next life than he ever did in this one.

THE BROOD

"Show me your anger and then I can understand it"
—Dr. Hal Raglan (Oliver Reed)

Without a shadow of a doubt, David Cronenberg's **The Brood** (1979) offers the most outrageous cadre for Reed to showcase his acting talents. Normality as we know it does not exist in the visionary universe of Cronenberg, populated as it is by eccentric characters, diverse theories, boundary-stretching philosophies and the director's trademark "body horror", where human flesh becomes the battleground of our assorted anxieties and neuroses.

In such a sensationalist setting, it is to Reed's considerable credit that he gives such an assured, understated performance of some subtlety, perfectly suited to the challenging source material. As Dr. Hal Raglan, Reed is the omnipotent head of the groundbreaking Somafree Institute of Psychoplasmics and the author of the best-selling book "The Shape Of Rage".

His singular treatment of his patients involves encouraging them to externalise their numerous internal rages and neuroses through intensive therapy sessions, forcing his patients to confront their own emotional crisis in order to affect a cure – so for psychoplasmics, read catharsis.

Unfortunately Raglan's treatment also being about a whole series of other, more disturbing side-effects and profound body changes. In the case of one disaffected patient Hartog (Robert Silverman), the treatment results in the manifestation of hideous exploded lymph sacs on his neck, and he resorts to suing Raglan for "urging his body to revolt against him".

"I've got a small revolution on my hands and I'm not putting it down very successfully," he explains. His aggrieved anti-Raglan slogan is "Psychoplasmics can cause cancer", a mantra also taken up by another patient's husband, Frank Carveth (Art Hindle): "Goddam it. Psychoplasmics is a rip-off. It's a sideshow. I've seen it in action".

Whilst Frank's anger is verbally manifested and Hartog's anger visibly manifested for all to see, Raglan's pet patient, Frank's estranged wife Nola (Samantha Eggar), externalises her anger vicariously through the grotesque dwarf children who are the product of her inner rage and who viciously bludgeon their chosen victims to death in a direct response to their "mother", Nola's, mood swings.

The Carveths' young daughter Candy (Cindy Hinds) is the innocent pawn caught up in the resulting emotional fall-out between the sceptic Frank and the believing Nola. This particular sub-plot has led to many critics dubbing **The Brood** rather ironically as Cronenberg's own unique take on the separation tear-jerker, **Kramer Versus Kramer** (also 1979). As Cronenberg himself revealed to John McCarthy in a 1984 interview: "It's sort of the nightmare side of that movie in which everyone was relatively polite, reasonable, understanding and compassionate".

Despite the surreal plot dynamics, Cronenberg's considerable directorial control enables him to handle the action at a compelling level of emotional intensity which also serves to channel into the human psyche's own passionate distrust of psychoanalysts and medical practices.

"Show me your anger, Nola. Show it to me," Raglan demands

of his favoured patient in one of their many intimate one-to-one therapy sessions where Raglan's continual role-playing includes acting both as Nola's daughter Candy, and as her father, who we discover didn't protect her as a father should his child during Nola's formative years – and it is this troubled past relationship in which Nola's present-day anger is firmly rooted.

Whereas the vicarious pleasures derived by the elderly couple in Michael Reeve's intriguing and comparable **The Sorcerers** (1967) are largely reactive, Cronenberg takes things a stage further in **The Brood** as Nola's mood swings and rage are positively proactive in providing the catalyst for the murderous actions of her "brood" children.

So, as her angst-level rises during childhood regression and the traumas it reveals, so we see Candy's grandmother Julianna (Nuala Fitzgerald) trying to shelter Candy in the family home as the food hatch in the kitchen is suddenly hammered on by unseen hands, milk is spilt and pots and pans fall en masse from their shelves and onto the floor. As Julianna goes to investigate, little red-coated killers emerge and batter her to death with mallets – blood splattering jarringly against the pristine white decor.

Later, as Raglan concentrates on Nola's father Barton Kelly (Henry Beckman) during their therapy session, the brood claim him as their next victim as his drunken body, collapsed on a bed, is suddenly engulfed by scaly hands from below as the red-coated assassins batter him to death with glass ornaments.

Having arrived just too late to save him, Frank does manage to capture one of the midgets and under scientific examination the absence of any naval on the child is noted – "That means that this creature has never really been born," the surgeon deduces pointedly, signposting the way for later real-life medical advances including the so-called "test-tube" babies where embryos are fertilised/born in a clinical rather than human environment.

Nola also directs her rage outwards towards Frank's friends when, mistakenly believing him to be having an affair with Candy's teacher, Ruth (Susan Hogan), the brood arrive at the school classroom and mete out their rough "justice" by stabbing the unfortunate teacher to death in front of the whole class – except, poignantly, Candy herself who is ushered away from the mayhem.

Again, it is Frank who arrives just too late to prevent the bloodshed – entering the class only to find the bloodied body of Ruth prone on the floor as all around, the sound of the children sobbing dominates the scene – Frank covering Ruth's disfigured face with a child's painting.

The peculiarly unsettling image of Candy being led along a snow-bound highway by two of the brood strikes a chilling note as the film veers towards its shocking denouement, centring on Raglan's isolated institute.

It is here that Frank confronts Raglan, who tries vainly to explain the complexities of the bizarre situation surrounding Nola and her brood: "She's not their surrogate mother Frank. She's their *real* mother. Their *only* mother". He continues despite Frank's look of disbelief: "They're her children Frank. More exactly they're the children of her rage. They're motivated only by her anger, whether it's conscious or unconscious."

This pivotal statement sets up the intriguing finale where Frank has to force himself to confront his wife and interact lovingly with her on an emotional level in order that Raglan can simultaneously snatch Candy safely from the clutches of the brood in the next outbuilding.

The sight of Nola, in her primal, clinical white dress, slowly rocking on her haunches, is suitably disquieting – as is her demeanour when Frank enters the room. "Are you ready for me

Frank? I seem to be in the middle of a strange adventure". With that, she lifts up her dress to reveal an enormous green foetal sac resting on her lap to the strains of Howard Shore's celebratory, uterine music. It's the salient moment not just from this particular film but, arguably, from Cronenberg's entire oeuvre, especially so as Nola stoops to bite open the sac with her bare teeth, whereupon a new child bloodily emerges.

If this scene alone wasn't highly-charged enough, the tension is twisted to almost unbearable levels as Cronenberg's artful inter-cutting between the dual action also includes Raglan's tip-toeing progress towards Candy, through the ever-watching, hissing brood children.

As Nola then proceeds to lick her newborn and Frank tries desperately to disguise his inner revulsion, she counters: "You hate me," with his denials shouted down thus: "You liar. You're lying!" she spits forth as we cut to the helpless Raglan, now being attacked by the rapidly enraged brood children.

"I'd kill Candice before I'd let you take her," Nola announces venomously as the brood now encircle the frightened Candy – bloodied hands banging repeatedly against the door she is hiding behind in one ironic Cronenberg nod to George Romero's similar scenes in **Night Of The Living Dead** (1968) and **Dawn Of The Dead** (1977).

As Frank moves quickly to strangle Nola, she collapses clutching her bloodied embryo to her side, he then races to the next building, stumbling past Raglan's battered corpse but thankfully finding Candy still alive, although crouched in terror in a corner.

The final ominous shot reveals Frank driving Candy away in his car, tears in her eyes but also, significantly, with two tell-tale blister marks on her arm to signal that the rage now continues in her young body.

As is so likely with Cronenberg's confrontational work, **The Brood** divided opinion severely with *The Times* extolling it in that "There is no denying David Cronenberg's growing skill at staging horror and producing the authentic frisson...", whilst others such as John Stanley in the "Creature Features Movies Guide Strikes Again" (Creatures At Large Press) finds it "An intriguing idea, but blatantly offensive", an inexplicable remark eclipsed however by Martin Sutton writing in "Movies Of The Seventies" (Orbis). He claims Cronenberg to be the "least interesting" (?!) of the "marginal" directors and whose works such as **The Brood**, **Rabid** and **Shivers** "reveal beneath their squalid nastiness an immature attitude towards sexuality and a misogynistic tendency as pronounced as Brian De Palma's". Misguided indeed!

As for Oliver Reed here, he invests his role with the calm authority required to mesmerise his flock – "he's a genius," one enrapt devotee gushes during (appropriately) a stage(d) performance of his therapeutic techniques, which veers from role-playing to patient humiliation on one swift move.

He displays the necessary arrogance of all "visionaries/pioneers", calmly styling his hair in the mirror as Frank berates his techniques in one of their many heated exchanges. He also retains the aloof nature required of his intellectual status here, and although his increasingly intimate counselling sessions with Nola suggest a sexual undercurrent, these remain implicit rather than explicit, unless you opt for the truly Cronenbergian theory that perhaps the brood children are the product of both Nola *and* Raglan, and that the rage expressed is not hers alone but also his, their energies mating and reproducing on the psychic level.

Either way, Reed gives a thoroughly convincing, flawless performance in what is somewhat unfamiliar territory for him, bordering on sci-fi in some respects, rendering his skill here to be even more consummate.

VENOM

"Look, this isn't just stealing cars you know. I mean, if something goes wrong they're going to lock us up and throw away the key"
—Dave (Oliver Reed) to Louise (Susan George)

Remembering the old adage for actors not to work with children and animals, what could be worse than suffering not just an animal-loving child, but an *exotic* animal-loving child. So, not for young Philip Hopkins (Lance Holcomb), a friendly furry cat or dog, but a slippery housesnake – transformed for artistic licence here in **Venom** (1982) to a deadly, highly venomous creature – no, not our friend Jaemel (Klaus Kinski), but a Black Mamba – deadliest of all snakes. What's your poison Olly, indeed.

Although intriguingly Tobe **The Texas Chain Saw Massacre** Hooper was originally slated to helm this 1982 exploitationer, it was finally Piers Haggard who took on the task of bringing this collision of genres – revenge of nature, heist and siege films – to the screen, aided by some sterling performances, notably from the snake (and yes, for all of you out there who are big on snake semantics, it is actually grey in colour not black, despite what the name suggests, with only the inside of the mouth being black).

With the grey cap and suited, moustached Olly as Dave the chauffeur and the coquettish Louise (Susan George) as the maid, the scene is soon set as the duo, along with Kinski's master criminal, broker their audacious plot to kidnap their young charge, Philip in return for a fat ransom fee from his wealthy parents.

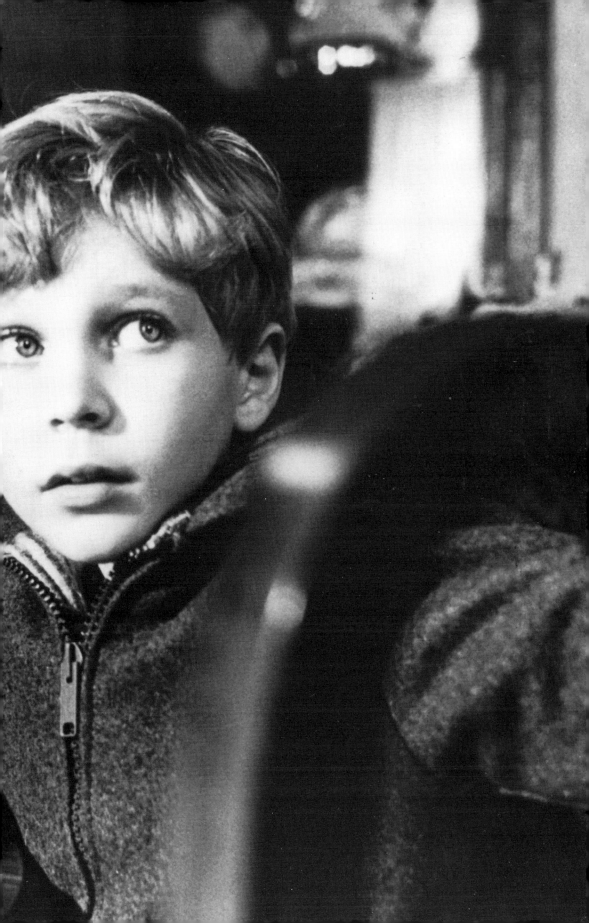

As dramatic expediency overtakes any artistic realism, the pet-loving Philip scuppers the would-be kidnappers scheming by deciding to add a harmless house-snake to his ever-expanding menagerie of household pets, only for it to be accidentally switched by the pet shop into a Black Mamba instead.

What is most fascinating here as the action unfolds is how the abrasive characters interact, injecting as much venom into each other as the deadly snake they are striving to elude.

Reed's bullying, brutish chauffeur prefers resorting to fists rather than any intellectual debate – "You make one sound and I'll put my foot through your stomach," being his threat to the boy's grandfather, ex-gamehunter Anderson (Sterling Hayden).

The tension between Dave and Jaemel is also palpable – rampant male egos battling for supremacy and also for the sultry Louise – her tantalising striptease from her maid's uniform to reveal her black lingerie underneath in front of a mesmerised Dave, is later counterpointed by her warm embrace with Jaemel who comments: "I don't like this chauffeur, this Dave. His hands sweat".

Dave's aggression and Jaemel's intellect are continually grating as Jaemel admonishes him for threatening their young hostage: "Don't touch the boy... you don't touch anyone unless I say so. I will tell you when to *breathe*".

Continuing this theme of inflated egos, Dave's subsequent shooting of a policeman outside the house, brings the full weight of the Metropolitan force to bear as they stake out the building, headed up by the unlikely figure of Commander

William Bulloch (Nicol Williamson) – "If any of our men talks above a whisper, I'll have his balls," being his curt threat.

Haggard, who also directed such diverse projects as the Peter Sellers vehicle **The Fiendish Plot Of Fu Manchu** (1980) and the worthy medieval horror **Blood On Satan's Claw** (1971) – which is memorable for some striking witchcraft/satanic imagery – handles the mamba's initial appearance with some aplomb. Shots of the grinning Philip picking up his crate and cradling it with considerable excitement, are inter-cut with herpetologist Dr. Marion Stowe (Sarah Miles) discovering that their new specimen snake at the London Institute of Toxicology is not a deadly mamba but a harmless house-snake.

When the crate is opened back at the house by Louise, she is bitten rapidly and repeatedly by the enraged mamba, the shots of the snake's head coiling and striking being most effective.

"I can't breathe," proves to be the unfortunate Louise's epitaph, although her final death throes veer on the side of "hammy" – thrashing around uncontrollably on a bed, her face pale and grey, sweating and blistered with a bleeding mouth.

Having then seen the snake slither away and attack Philip's remaining pets before then disappearing into the air vent, the siege proper now begins and the tension mounts between Dave and Jaemel, with the continual menace of the mamba lurking in the background as Anderson's experience as a big game hunter is drawn upon when he is ordered to search for the reptile.

The implicit fear as to whether that electrical lead or displaced coal scuttle lid is, or contains the mamba, makes for a taut atmosphere amongst the rather one-dimensional character posturing, and adds a real air of tension to the action.

This is heightened in traditional genre fashion as Miles' herpetologist utters a chilling warning whilst simultaneously extolling the creature's main attributes: "They're extraordinary creatures. Very nervous, terribly unpredictable. Paranoid really. In a confined space like that they'll attack just whenever they can. They're also the fastest snakes in the world. They're capable of launching themselves bodily – ten to fifteen feet through the air. They strike so fast that nobody could possibly get away". As if this wasn't ominous enough, the doctor continues: "In all the case studies we know of, mamba bites are one hundred per cent fatal." Know thy enemy indeed.

Inside the confines of the house, Jaemel continues to keep his cool whilst the volatile Dave continues to lose his – "I'm sick to bloody death of you telling me what to do," he spits venomously at Jaemel, similarly betraying little sense of sympathy for the asthma-suffering Philip – "Look, who gives a damn if the boy dies or not, they're not going to know about that outside are they?" he shouts callously to Anderson.

Only when Jaemel dupes Dr. Stowe into entering the house under the pretext of administering a serum to the maid (the police aren't aware she has died from the snake-bite injuries she sustained), does Dave offer any semblance of compassion, by offering a stiff drink to the rather shaken doctor. Even then however, his violent tendencies and primal instinct for self-preservation rears its head like the hissing mamba which uncoils from the back of the drinks cabinet to his utmost horror.

As Bulloch and his men, fearing increasingly for the lives of the hostages, set about breaking into the building via a bricked-up basement access door, **Venom** slithers headlong into its kinetic finale.

Having failed in stopping Bulloch bursting through into the basement, Dave is left lying on the floor, dazed and bleeding from a gunshot wound. As he slowly crawls up the staircase with a supreme effort, he hears a trademark hiss and turns around slowly only to see the mamba on the floor below him, near to his foot. As the perspiration runs down his forehead, Dave watches agonisingly as the mamba crawls ever so s-l-o-w-l-y up his trouser leg – his death screams as he is bitten skilfully intercut with the screams of Philip's mother Ruth (Cornelia Sharpe) upon returning from abroad and discovering her son's plight. Having lived by the sword, Dave also dies by the sword, his extreme death by snakebite agonisingly felt by the (male) audience all the same.

Having now dispensed of two of the evil kidnapping triumvirate, the mamba then makes its way towards Jaemel upstairs – as Jaemel struggles in vain with the snake, they become entangled in one of the window drapes and both plunge dramatically out of the upstairs window – Kinski's overacting here has to be seen to be believed and is almost as if competing with George for the most scenery-chewing demise. As if the frenzied mamba strikes are not enough, a police marksman's bullet also finds its way into Jaemel's falling body, leaving him motionless on the pavement below and swathed in a now bloodied drape – it's certainly an appropriate way of taking the final curtain!

The final, ironic closing sequence hints strongly that the slithering terror is not yet over as small baby mambas are revealed, crawling out of their eggs near a heater in the house.

Although the film met with some critical "venom" of its own upon its release with the likes of Leonard Maltin dismissing it as "Half the big-name cast appears to be drunk, the other half looks as though it wishes it were. Destined to become a camp classic", Haggard's film is engaging enough and given an added gusto by the bravura performances. **Venom** was clearly never going to be challenging for any "gongs" but the mamba itself proves to be a suitably fearsome adversary and both Reed and Kinski probably give the script more than it is really worth with professional, committed performances. (Olly, of course, would once more tussle with a murderous snake in **Spasms**, in 1983.)

For Oliver Reed, his career roles have often straddled the tightrope of playing on the one hand, smooth, urbane charmers and on the other, loveable rogues sometimes venturing into complete thugs; and his role as the frustrated, emotionally-charged chauffeur in **Venom** is rooted firmly in the latter territory. Sadly, after his notable role in David Cronenberg's **The Brood**, his career was already starting on the downward slope, with only the odd film of any note (such as **Castaway**) to come. More and more, he was to become a celebrity known more for his hell-raising antics in bars across the world, plus various drunken appearances on television, than as the fine actor he undoubtedly was.

CASTAWAY

"My brain is like my prick, it goes up and down of its own accord and sometimes it explodes with excitement. And when you see it lying there, doing nothing, nothing at all, then you'd be surprised what it's capable of thinking."
—Gerald Kingsland (Oliver Reed)

Based on Lucy Irvine's book of the same name, **Castaway** (1987), ably directed with his usual visual élan by Nicolas Roeg, offers an intriguing view on personal relationships as a middle-aged man, Gerald (Oliver Reed), advertises in *Time Out* magazine for a "wife to join him on a desert island for one year". When Lucy (Amanda Donohoe) replies, perhaps seeking to escape her humdrum existence working in a tax office as much as seeking a taste for adventure, a whirlwind series of candle-lit dinners ensues before they inevitably end up in bed together.

Their decidedly practical rather than romantic "courtship" is accentuated in the hastily arranged marriage ceremony in a London registry office, to be followed by a Chinese takeaway!

Next we see them transported onto a boat, traversing the azure blue waters to the sun-kissed island that is to be their new home for the next year. Although their new-found surroundings are suitably idyllic, it soon becomes apparent that this is something that Gerald and Lucy's own relationship will never be, as the harsh realities of everyday life – namely, building a shelter and searching for food – eclipse the visual utopia they are inhabiting.

Gerald's hedonistic, chauvinistic approach is basically to lie in the sun for as long as possible, preferably ogling Lucy's lithe form – which remains at least semi-naked, if not naked, for most of the time – and hoping for a passionate sex session at every opportunity.

Whilst all this may well represent Gerald's idea of desert island heaven, it certainly doesn't concur with Lucy's more practical approach to life. For her, she seeks the challenge of not merely surviving on their dream haven, but positively flourishing. To her, their survival is a personal challenge and her own ambitions drive her to reach out beyond this and guarantee their happiness through having a real sense of purpose and achievement.

The die is cast however, on their very first night out under the stars as they cuddle intimately in their tent, only for the whole romantic ambience to be shattered by Gerald having forgotten to load the extra supplies of iodine and flour onto their utility boat before landing on the island. "I'm randy," he later purrs – with "Stop it!" being the ice cold response.

When they later venture out on one of their numerous food-hunting sorties, Gerald is quick to seize the opportunity for having an impromptu rest in the midst of the dense inland jungle terrain – "You lazy sod. You've just found another excuse to sit down. You're always lying about," Lucy chastises him.

In an attempt to placate her, Gerald begins planting his own garden in order to help sustain them and add some self-sufficiency to their diet – "Our lives may depend upon these vegetables," he ventures dramatically to her.

When, during another food-finding mission, Gerald is attacked and badly stung by irate bees, Lucy tends to his reddening, blistered legs – "When you wrote answering the ad, is this what you expected?" Gerald asks, her frustration at their current situation supplying his rhetorical answer. For Lucy, the dream has been all, and has differed sharply from the reality thus far.

With Gerald's equally volatile temper and mood swings

similarly in evidence, their sniping at each other continues with some venom – "God, it frightens me your anger, when we're here on this island alone," Lucy announces; "You're a smug little shit," being Gerald's vitriolic reply. He continues that: "Nothing's changed here. I didn't get fat or bald or forget to wash behind my ears did I? Nothing's changed here except you girl... you lied and you wormed your way down here. Well, we've got nine months and twenty-six days to go. Let's see if we can both last that long shall we?"

Lucy wanders off to find her own "space" on the other side of the island and to escape Gerald's crude and infantile limericks. When they are finally reunited she again has to administer to his now haemorrhaging sores, and also glimpses the green shoots now apparent in his garden. No such embryonic signs of recovery in their relationship emerge however, as Gerald continues to expound his uniquely coarse philosophy; "A screw and a cold beer is the summit of my ambition now. You could found a whole new religion on this island with a screw and a cold beer." He adds ironically; "Lucy, I said *screw* not stew," as she serves him his meal.

His "philosophical" side now well and truly to the fore, Gerald offers his considered thoughts on the battle of the sexes, explaining how: "Women love to skewer us, figure us out and pigeon-hole us. 'He's reliable, he's quiet but gentle, he's sweet with kids – I really do know the inner him' they say to themselves, nodding wisely. And they're amazed when suddenly he breaks rank and they didn't know diddly-shit about him."

Their intense, inner circle of anguish is then momentarily breached by a duo of athletic Aussies (!) who land on the island under the pretext of handing out census forms (!) to the occupants. As Gerald compares his own unshaven, ageing and blistered appearance with the rippling, unblemished muscles of Jason (Tony Rickards) and Rod (Todd Rippon), his envy is all too apparent, and he is keen to bid adieu to them as soon as is humanly possible. "Cover your tits for God's sake, cover your tits," being Gerald's immediate response to Lucy when the visitors arrive.

For Lucy however, the prospect of more scintillating

conversation (and flirtation) is appealing – now it is she who reclines as the patient, as her new suitors rub ointment into her sores, before setting off on a sun-kissed walk across the stunning rock formations which characterise the island. Whilst indulging her young companions, she confesses her frustrations with Gerald – "I suppose it's because he's older than me," she volunteers having bemoaned his (perceived at least) lack of imagination. As the new visitors so acutely observe however, it is Gerald and Lucy's exclusive proximity to one another – the claustrophobia inherent in their isolated situation – which renders love impossible. They are with each other every waking hour with no other outlets, no other friends. Whilst the truth is of paramount importance in any relationship, Gerald and Lucy have no option, no opportunity for innocent flirtation or harmless mystery and intrigue. It is upon this stifling intimacy that any chance for *real* intimacy flounders.

"I had to defend you. I was so ashamed," Lucy admonishes Gerald as the visitors finally leave. "You bloody threw yourself at them like some randy bloody bitch," Gerald venomously spits back at her.

As their argument intensifies, Lucy defines the cusp of the problem for her as being: "Look at this place Gerald. Look at what we've done here. Look at what *you've* done here – nothing," as she surveys the primitive shelter he has "constructed".

With their crumbling "marriage" now eroded like the strident rocks upon the island which are continually buffeted by the sea, we see the lack of fresh water supplies beginning to stifle their vegetable garden, Gerald's sores becoming septic and Lucy almost dying – vomiting after eating some poisonous fruit.

Roeg's masterly vision captures an almost "still-life" shot of Gerald and Lucy, lying naked together with bones protruding from beneath their now emaciated bodies, like some horrific concentration camp victims, simultaneously both dreaming of happier times in the hustle, bustle and *civilisation* of London.

At this low ebb, they then prove that the darkest hour really is before the dawn – which arrives, bringing with it salvation

in the unlikely guise of two nuns emerging from an outboard motor-boat – Sister Saint Margaret (Georgina Hale) and Sister Saint Winifred (Frances Barber), who are able to give them immediate medical attention.

Physical health now on the mend, mental health and self-esteem is likewise restored to Gerald as he seeks to indulge in his motor vehicle repair skills, having been invited over by the locals from the next island – as Lucy ironically observes: "He's so absorbed that he's almost forgotten to remind me of the uselessness of being a cunt that doesn't fuck – but not quite."

Even Gerald's new found craftsmanship doesn't solve their personal problems however, as Lucy becomes upset at becoming a "mechanic's widow", with Gerald also disappearing overnight on some occasions. "Maybe if there was some sex here then I wouldn't have to keep buggering off," he retorts, whereupon a surreal encounter unfolds as Lucy – clad in intricate lace bra and stockings – agrees to Gerald's wish. Even the virulent storm which strikes the island, completely devastating their home, cannot interrupt this coitus and the next morning, they are still locked together in embrace as the ruins of their "home" lies around them.

The final scenes see Gerald deciding to stay on the island with Lucy departing on a charter plane and, presumably, back to the urban sprawl and civilisation of London.

Probably the most fascinating aspect of **Castaway** is how it uncovers the different facets of a personal relationship and in particular, the difficulty in marrying up our ambitions and our needs with those of our partners. The very characteristics which attract Lucy to Gerald initially – his boldness, his jokey, irreverent humour and his extrovert nature – become the characteristics which she begins to hate when transferred from urban London to an isolated desert island.

Although their initial struggles on the new island suggest that it is Lucy who has the greater resolve and determination to survive and succeed rather than Gerald, it is ultimately Gerald who finally appears at one with himself, content with his way of life and how he is living it, whilst it is Lucy who jets back to the safe existence that she knows best.

Their whirlwind introductions in London and rapid marriage and change of life basically made no allowance for any real understanding of each other's aspirations and innermost feelings as, ironically, their very *closeness* proves to be the catalyst for their eventual separation. Everything here is made in paradise; unfortunately however, its occupants betray only too well the particular personality traits and contrasting character foibles which constitute the flawed human race, compressed into 12 months of bitter conflict.

Both Reed and Donohoe imbue their roles with a considerable gusto as they set about the daily struggle for survival in their modern day Robinson Crusoe existence, ably supported by Roeg's all-consuming camera which breathes in every ounce of beauty the island's natural splendour allows for, greedily devouring the idyllic surroundings, especially in the numerous underwater sequences where ripples bubble through the ocean waters, spiralling ever upwards to the surface and the omnipresent sun which soars high overhead.

Oliver Reed's performance in **Castaway** is almost certainly the best from the latter part of his career. He lost a substantial amount of weight to play the part of Gerald (no doubt by means of one of his infamous "vodka diets"!), and seems completely at home in the role. Despite his facility in playing a drunken boor, however, Reed also introduces the deeper, sensitive side of Gerald by increments, subtly communicating Gerald's own particular unhappiness and frustrations. His physical presence is also impressive, conveying power and vitality even in the face of starvation.

FILMOGRAPHY

Gladiator (1999)
Jeremiah (1998, TV)
Marco Polo (1998)
Parting Shots (1998)
The Bruce (1996)
Funny Bones (1995)
Return To Lonesome Dove (1993, TV)
Severed Ties (1992)
Prisoner Of Honour (1991, TV)
Hired To Kill (1991)
A Ghost In Monte Carlo (1990, TV)
Treasure Island (1990, TV)
Panama Sugar (1990)
The Pit And The Pendulum (1990)
The Lady And The Highwayman (1989, TV)
The Return Of The Musketeers (1989)
The Revenger (1989)
The Adventures Of Baron Munchausen
       (1988)
Blind Justice (1988)
Captive Rage (1988)
Gor (1988)
The House Of Usher (1988)
Castaway (1987)
Master Of Dragonard Hill (1987)
The Misfit Brigade (1987)
Rage To Kill (1987)
Skeleton Coast (1987)
Captive (1986)
Christopher Columbus (1985, TV)
Black Arrow (1985, TV)
Spasms (1983)
Fanny Hill (1983)
The Sting II (1983)
Two Of A Kind (1983)
Venom (1982)
Condorman (1981)
Dr. Heckyl And Mr. Hype (1980)
Lion Of The Desert (1980)
The Brood (1979)
A Touch Of The Sun (1979)
The Big Sleep (1978)
Tomorrow Never Comes (1978)
The Class Of Miss MacMichael (1978)
Crossed Swords (1978)
Ransom (1977)
The Great Scout And Cathouse Thursday
       (1976)
The Sell-Out (1976)
Burnt Offerings (1976)
Royal Flash (1975)

Tommy (1975)
Lisztomania (1975)
The Four Musketeers (1974)
Ten Little Indians (1974)
Mahler (1974)
The Three Musketeers (1973)
Days Of Fury (1973)
Blue Blood (1973)
Mordi E Fuggi (1973)
Revolver (1973)
Triple Echo (1973)
Sitting Target (1972)
Dirty Weekend (1972)
Z.P.G. (1972)
The Hunting Party (1971)
The Devils (1971)
The Lady In The Car With Glasses And A
       Gun (1970)
Take A Girl Like You (1970)
Hannibal Brooks (1969)
The Assassination Bureau (1969)
Women In Love (1969)
Oliver! (1968)
Dante's Inferno (1967, TV)
I'll Never Forget What's'is Name (1967)
The Shuttered Room (1967)
The Jokers (1967)
The Debussy Film (1966, TV)
The Party's Over (1966)
The System (1966)
The Trap (1966)
The Brigand Of Kandahar (1965)
The Damned (1963)
Paranoiac (1963)
The Crimson Blade (1963)
Pirates Of Blood River (1962)
Captain Clegg (1962)
The Curse Of The Werewolf (1961)
His And Hers (1961)
No Love For Johnnie (1961)
The Rebel (1961)
The Two Faces Of Dr. Jekyll (1960)
Beat Girl (1960)
The Angry Silence (1960)
The Bulldog Breed (1960)
Sword Of Sherwood Forest (1960)
The League Of Gentlemen (1959)
The Captain's Table (1958)
The Square Peg (1958)
Hello London (1958)